Low-c...

safe, punctual, ecological,
economic, uniting people,
redundant....

INTRODUCTION	**12**
HOW DID THEY COME INTO BEING?	**12**
HISTORY OF LCC IN EUROPE	**14**
ORIGINS AND PIONEERS	14
MICHAEL O'LEARY - MARKETING GENIUS	16
STELIOS HAJI-IOANNOU - THE DIVERSIFIER	17
BJØRN KJOS - THE INNOVATOR	17
JÓZSEF VÁRADI - THE STRATEGIST	17
EXPANSION AND INTERNATIONALISATION	**18**
TECHNOLOGICAL DEVELOPMENTS	18
PARTNERSHIPS AND ALLIANCES	18
POLITICAL STABILITY AND UNIFORM REGULATIONS	19
PUBLIC PERCEPTION AND BRAND IDENTITY	19
COST EFFICIENCY AND ECONOMIES OF SCALE	19
RESPONDING TO THE COMPETITIVE LANDSCAPE	19
WHAT ROLE DID EU ENLARGEMENT PLAY?	**20**
INCREASING THE POTENTIAL FOR MARKET EXPANSION	20
UNIFICATION OF REGULATIONS AND OPEN SKIES AGREEMENT	20
ECONOMIC INTEGRATION AND INCREASING MOBILITY	21
INCENTIVES AND SUBSIDIES	21
CHANGING THE COMPETITIVE LANDSCAPE	21
DEVELOPMENT OF CONSUMER AWARENESS	21
INCREASE IN CROSS-BORDER SERVICES	22
STANDARDISATION OF CONSUMER PROTECTION RULES	22
DEVELOPMENT OF THE INFRASTRUCTURE NETWORK	22
CULTURAL DIVERSITY AND TRAVEL TRENDS	22
GEOPOLITICAL CONSIDERATIONS	23
INFLUENCE ON PRICE STRUCTURES AND COMPETITIVENESS	23
KEY MOMENTS	**23**
DEREGULATION IN THE 1990S	23
ATTACKS OF 11 SEPTEMBER 2001	24

OUTBREAK OF THE GLOBAL FINANCIAL CRISIS IN 2008	24
RISE OF THE ONLINE BOOKING PLATFORMS	24
ENVIRONMENTAL AWARENESS AND SUSTAINABILITY MOVEMENTS	25
COVID 19 PANDEMIC	25
HOW HAVE CRISES AFFECTED THE INDUSTRY?	25

COSTS 26

FUEL COSTS: THE HEART OF OPERATIONS	27
PERSONNEL COSTS: MORE THAN JUST SALARIES	27
AIRPORT AND LANDING FEES	27
MAINTENANCE AND SERVICING	28
MARKETING AND SALES: DIGITAL STRATEGIES	28
CATERING AND ON-BOARD SERVICES	28
INSURANCE: A NECESSARY EVIL	28
LEASING AND DEPRECIATION: A BALANCING ACT	29
WHAT ROLE DOES OUTSOURCING PLAY?	29
GROUND HANDLING	29
MAINTENANCE	30
CUSTOMER SERVICE	30
IT SERVICES	30
CATERING AND ON-BOARD SERVICES	30
PERSONNEL	31
ULTRA LOW COST CARRIER	31

REVENUE SOURCES 34

TICKET SALES: THE MAIN REVENUE GENERATOR	34
ONBOARD SALES	35
PARTNERSHIPS AND COOPERATION	35
ADVERTISING	35
FREIGHT AND LOGISTICS SERVICES	35

DYNAMIC PRICING	36
ANNUAL OR SUBSCRIPTION MODELS	36
SALE OF CUSTOMER DATA	36
ADDITIONAL FEES	37
BAGGAGE FEES	37
FEES FOR SEAT SELECTION	37
PRIORITY BOARDING	37
AMENDMENT AND CANCELLATION FEES	38
FOOD AND DRINKS ON BOARD	38
AIRPORT CHECK-IN FEES	38
SUPPLEMENTARY INSURANCE AND SERVICE PACKAGES	38
FEES FOR SPECIAL BAGGAGE	39

PARTNERSHIPS 39

RISK MANAGEMENT 40

MARKET RISKS 41

FUEL PRICES 42

FUEL PRICE HEDGING (FUEL HEDGING)	43
FUTURES AND FORWARDS	43
OPTIONS	43
SWAPS	44
OVER-THE-COUNTER (OTC) DERIVATIVES	44
EFFICIENT FLEET MANAGEMENT	44
FLEXIBLE ROUTING AND ROUTE PLANNING	45
DYNAMIC PRICING	45
OPERATIONAL ADJUSTMENTS	45
MULTI-SOURCE APPROACH	45
PASS-THROUGH CLAUSES	46

THE PLAYERS — 46

- Ryanair — 46
- EasyJet — 47
- Wizz Air — 47
- Norwegian Air Shuttle — 47
- Vueling — 47
- Eurowings — 47
- Transavia — 48
- Laudamotion — 48
- Pegasus Airlines — 48
- Jet2.com — 48
- TUI fly — 48
- Level — 49
- Smartwings — 49
- AirBaltic — 49
- Volotea — 49
- SunExpress — 49
- FlyPlay — 50

WHAT DISTINGUISHES THE LCC? — 50

- Business models — 51
- Geographical orientation — 51
- Range of services — 51
- Market niches and specialities — 52
- Aircraft fleet — 52
- Customer relationship and brand image — 52
- Price structure — 53

SMALLER AND REGIONAL LCC — 53

REGIONAL FLIGHTS AND SMALL TOWNS	54
ETHNIC OR CULTURAL CONNECTIONS	55
BUSINESS CITY CONNECTIONS	55
SEASONAL FLIGHTS	55
NICHE HOLIDAY DESTINATIONS	56
ECO-FOCUS	56
COMBINED TRAVEL PACKAGES	56
SPECIAL OFFERS FOR STUDENTS AND YOUNG TRAVELLERS	56
LUXURY CHEAP FLIGHTS	57

STRATEGIC ALLIANCES 57

GLOBAL ALLIANCES	57
CODESHARE AGREEMENTS	58
JOINT VENTURES	58
STRATEGIC INVESTMENTS	59
SPECIALISED ALLIANCES	59
TECHNOLOGICAL PARTNERSHIPS	59
RESPONSE TO CRISES	59
ALLIANCES OF LCCs	60
CODESHARE AND INTERLINING AGREEMENTS	60
JOINT PURCHASING STRATEGIES	60
OPERATING COOPERATIONS	60
FRANCHISE AND LICENSING MODELS	61
MARKETING AND ADVERTISING PARTNERSHIPS	61
DIGITAL PLATFORMS AND BOOKING SYSTEMS	61
STRATEGIC PARTICIPATIONS	61

REGULATIONS AND LEGISLATION 63

FLIGHT SAFETY	63
ENVIRONMENTAL PROTECTION	64

CONSUMER PROTECTION	**64**
MARKET ACCESS AND COMPETITION	**65**
OPEN SKIES AGREEMENT	65
RESTRAINTS OF COMPETITION	66
LABOUR LAW	66
SECURITY AND SURVEILLANCE	66
EU LAW	**67**
MARKET LIBERALISATION AND COMPETITION	67
AIR PASSENGER RIGHTS	67
ENVIRONMENTAL PROTECTION	67
SAFETY STANDARDS	67
LABOUR LAW AND SOCIAL STANDARDS	68
DATA PROTECTION	68
ADDITIONAL FEES AND TRANSPARENCY	68
SLOT REGULATION	68
CABOTAGE RIGHTS	69
GEOBLOCKING	69
BREXIT AND ITS EFFECTS	69
TAXES AND DUTIES	69
FUTURE REGULATIONS	70
SAFETY STANDARDS	**70**
AIRCRAFT CERTIFICATION	71
OPERATING PROCEDURES	71
CREW TRAINING	71
AIR TRAFFIC MANAGEMENT	71
AIRPORT SECURITY	71
COMMUNICATION	72
EMERGENCY PLANS	72
MONITORING AND AUDITS	72
DIFFERENCES TO TRADITIONAL AIRLINES	73
OPERATING MODELS	73
TURNAROUND TIMES	73
CREW RESOURCES	74

USE OF OLDER AIRCRAFT	74
ECONOMIC CONSIDERATIONS	74
SAFETY RECORD OF LOW-COST AIRLINES?	74
FACTORS INFLUENCING THE SAFETY RECORD	75
STATISTICAL DATA	75
MEDIA COVERAGE	76
ENVIRONMENTAL LAWS	**76**
EMISSION STANDARDS	76
NOISE REGULATIONS	77
FLIGHT ROUTES AND AIRSPACE USE	77
CO_2 COMPENSATION AND EMISSIONS TRADING	77
RENEWABLE ENERGIES AND SUSTAINABLE FUELS	77
WASTE MANAGEMENT	77
HOW IS THE AIRLINES' CARBON FOOTPRINT REGULATED?	**78**
INTERNATIONAL AGREEMENTS	78
EU EMISSIONS TRADING SCHEME (ETS)	79
NATIONAL REGULATIONS	79
INDUSTRY INITIATIVES	79
TRANSPARENCY AND REPORTING	79
SANCTIONS AND INCENTIVES	80
COMPETITION AND MARKET DYNAMICS	**80**
PRICE WARS	**80**
MERGERS AND ACQUISITIONS	**83**
BOOKING PLATFORMS OR APPS?	**86**
BOOKING PLATFORMS	86
APPS	87
FLEXIBILITY IN BOOKING	88
IN-FLIGHT EXPERIENCE	**88**
CUSTOMER INTERACTION AND SERVICE	**89**
QUALITY OF IN-FLIGHT CATERING AND OTHER SERVICES	**90**
BEFORE THE FLIGHT	**91**

CUSTOMER REVIEWS	91
SOCIAL MEDIA AND INFLUENCERS	93

ECONOMIC AND SOCIAL IMPACTS OF LCC — 94

TOURISM	94
IMPACT ON LOCAL ECONOMIES AND TOURISM INDUSTRY	96

WORKING CONDITIONS IN INDUSTRY — 97

EMPLOYMENT MODELS AND WORKERS' RIGHTS	97
WAGES AND BENEFITS	98
WORKING HOURS AND REST PERIODS	98
TRADE UNION REPRESENTATION	98
HEALTH AND SAFETY	98
LEGAL FRAMEWORK	99
TRAINING AND QUALIFICATION OPPORTUNITIES	99
GEOGRAPHICAL MOBILITY	99
DISCRIMINATION AND DIVERSITY	100
PSYCHOLOGICAL FACTORS	100
JOB SECURITY	100

ETHICS AND CRITICISM — 101

DISCUSSION ON ENVIRONMENTALLY HARMFUL PRACTICES	101
PUBLIC PERCEPTION	101
POLICY MEASURES	102
CORPORATE STRATEGIES	102
SOCIAL DISCOURSE	102
FUTURE CHALLENGES	103
SOCIAL AND CULTURAL CHANGES	103
DEMOCRATISATION OF TRAVEL	103

CHANGE IN LEISURE TIME ACTIVITIES	104
EFFECTS ON IDENTITY	104
SOCIAL IMPACT	104
CULTURAL HOMOGENISATION	105
GLOBALISATION OF THE MIDDLE CLASS	105
POLITICAL IMPACT	105
CHANGING RELATIONSHIP TO DISTANCES	105
INFLUENCING SELF-ESTEEM	106
GENERATIONAL DIFFERENCES	106
EDUCATION AND TOLERANCE	106

SURVIVAL STRATEGIES 107

SUSTAINABILITY	107
FUTURE REGULATIONS AND LAWS	109
CLIMATE PROTECTION LAWS	109
CONSUMER PROTECTION	110
INTERNATIONAL AIR TRAFFIC	110
DATA PROTECTION	110
LABOUR LAW	111
REGIONAL POLICY AND SUBSIDIES	111
SUSTAINABILITY GOALS AND SOCIAL RESPONSIBILITY	111
POST-COVID 19 TRENDS	112

WHAT DOES THE FUTURE LOOK LIKE? 114

LOW-COST STRATEGY OF CONVENTIONAL AIRLINES	114
NEWCOMERS FROM NON-EU COUNTRIES	115
LONG DISTANCE	117
POTENTIAL DISRUPTORS AND THEIR STRATEGIES	118
USE OF TECHNOLOGY	118
RADICAL COST REDUCTION	119

NETWORKING AND DATA USE	119
MULTIMODAL TRANSPORT SOLUTIONS	119
DECENTRALISATION AND LOCALISATION	119
CHANGE IN DISTRIBUTION CHANNELS	120
PARTNERSHIPS OUTSIDE THE INDUSTRY	120
SOCIAL AND ENVIRONMENTAL RESPONSIBILITY	120
DIRECT CUSTOMER INTERACTION	120
ADAPTABILITY AND AGILITY	120
SHIFT TO RAIL	121
CONCLUSION AND OUTLOOK	**122**

Introduction

A low-cost airline, often referred to as a low-cost carrier (LCC) or discount airline, is an airline that specialises in selling airline tickets at significantly lower prices than traditional airlines. In order to keep costs low and pass these savings on to customers, LCCs follow a number of business strategies and practices that differ from the methods of traditional airlines. In individual cases, the distinction from traditional airlines is not always clear.

LCCs often offer very limited in-flight amenities, for example in terms of catering, seat selection or entertainment systems. These airlines often fly to smaller or secondary airports that are less busy and therefore have lower landing fees. LCCs aim to get their flights as full as possible to reduce operating costs per passenger.

The fare structure is often kept very simple and there are only a few different ticket types. Aircraft are on the ground for as short a time as possible to minimise operating costs. Many LCCs use only one type of aircraft, which simplifies maintenance and staff training.

How did they come into being?

The history of LCCs is closely linked to the USA and the deregulation of the air transport market there and the rise of entrepreneurs who recognised the opportunity to offer cost-effective air services. Deregulation was introduced in 1978 with the Airline Deregulation Act. Until then, airline prices and routes were controlled by the government. Deregulation created a competitive market that enabled new and existing airlines to offer their services more flexibly and cost-efficiently.

The first notable low-cost airline in the US was Southwest Airlines, which began operations in 1971. Founded by Herb Kelleher, the airline relied on a simple business model characterised by a single aircraft type class, high turnaround times and point-to-point flights. This meant that Southwest offered direct flights instead of hub-and-spoke models, which meant that there was less ground time and thus costs were saved. In addition, there was a special focus on customer satisfaction, which helped the airline build a loyal customer base.

Over the years, other low-cost carriers such as JetBlue, Spirit Airlines and Frontier Airlines followed, each developing their own business models and strategies. For example, JetBlue introduced amenities such as in-flight entertainment and more comfortable seats to differentiate itself from competitors, while Spirit Airlines went for the ultra-low-cost model, where almost everything, from baggage to in-flight meals, cost extra.

The introduction of LCCs also led to changes in the established, traditional airlines. To compete with the lower prices of LCCs, airlines such as Delta, American and United developed their own "basic economy" fares, which offer fewer amenities but are also cheaper.

However, LCCs also faced challenges, particularly around cost efficiency and the need to make a profit while keeping prices low. These included volatile fuel prices, labour costs and regulatory hurdles. Nevertheless, they have managed to make air travel accessible to a wider population and fundamentally change the way people travel.

History of LCC in Europe

Origins and pioneers

How did LCCs get their start in Europe?

An important aspect in the development of LCCs has been the role of technology. Online booking systems, which became popular in the early 2000s, were crucial to the success of these airlines. By eliminating travel agents and other middlemen, they were able to further reduce costs and interact more directly with customers. This was not only cost-efficient, but also gave the airlines valuable data about customer preferences. They also used advanced algorithms for dynamic pricing, which enabled them to maximise the capacity utilisation of flights.

The role of regional airports

As mentioned earlier, smaller, often less frequented airports played a crucial role. These airports were only too happy to offer incentives to LCCs to generate more traffic and thus more revenue for the local economy. This often resulted in a win-win situation, with both the airlines and the airports and associated communities benefiting. Losers were and are some of the large airports.

Reactions of the incumbent airlines

The establishment of LCCs was a wake-up call for the traditional airlines. Many initially tried to drive the new competitors out of the market by cutting prices, but this often failed as their cost structures were much higher. Some established airlines later launched their own low-cost brands or adapted their service offerings to remain competitive.

LCCs not only revolutionised the European aviation market, but also influenced European culture and lifestyles. Weekend trips to other countries became common, and the Erasmus programme and other exchange initiatives became more accessible with cheaper flight options. This led to increased European integration, both economically and culturally.

The low-cost airline industry has not been without controversy. Issues of sustainability and working conditions for airline staff have gained prominence in recent years. While the low price of flying has given more people access to air travel, it has also increased CO_2 emissions and thus environmental pollution. In addition, there are criticisms regarding working conditions, as many of these airlines offer strict contract terms and lower wages compared to traditional airlines.

The way to the future

Although LCCs have experienced tough times several times, such as the 2008 financial crisis or the COVID 19 pandemic, they showed amazing resilience and adaptability. Their business model proved flexible enough to adapt to new market conditions, which only reinforced their importance in the European travel sector.

In retrospect, the beginnings of LCCs in Europe have fundamentally changed the landscape of European air transport and in many ways democratised it. Although they face a number of challenges and criticisms, they remain a central part of the European transport infrastructure and an interesting example of free market dynamics.

Who are the key people behind the first LCCs?

Michael O'Leary - Marketing Genius

Michael O'Leary, the man behind Ryanair, has not only made a difference by cutting costs, but also by his marketing skills. He has always made polarising but media-savvy proposals, such as charging for toilet use or cutting down on the co-pilot, which were never implemented but kept the Ryanair brand constantly in the headlines. This kept Ryanair in the conversation and attracted considerable attention, which ultimately led to an increase in bookings.

Stelios Haji-Ioannou - The Diversifier

Stelios Haji-Ioannou went beyond the airline industry with EasyJet and founded the "EasyGroup", which moved into various business areas such as hotels, car rentals and even food. His approach to diversify the "Easy" brand shows his entrepreneurial zeal and drive to take the low-cost idea into different industries.

Bjørn Kjos - The Innovator

Bjørn Kjos' decision to integrate long-haul flights into the low-cost model was a bold move and brought Norwegian Air into focus as one of the most innovative airlines in Europe. By using fuel-efficient aircraft such as the Boeing 787 Dreamliner, he was able to keep costs down while making long-haul travel affordable. Unfortunately, this long-haul model ultimately did not prove viable (yet?).

József Váradi - The Strategist

József Váradi used the lack of low-cost flight offers in Central and Eastern Europe to his advantage. By focusing on this region, Wizz Air was able to achieve steady growth and capture market share from traditional airlines. He also positioned Wizz Air as one of the first European airlines to aggressively expand into the Ukrainian and other Eastern European markets to gain a leading position.

What all these key individuals, and many others, have in common is their ability to challenge and radically change established business models and practices.

Whether it is marketing tactics, aircraft types, geographic focus areas or even industry diversification, these individuals have proven that the will to innovate and take risks is essential in the dynamic world of aviation. Their influence is not limited to the companies they have led, but has revolutionised the industry as a whole and changed access to travel for millions of people.

Expansion and internationalisation

How have LCCs spread across Europe's national borders?

Technological developments

The rapid development of technologies, especially the internet, has greatly facilitated the cross-border expansion of LCCs. Online booking platforms and mobile apps have enabled airlines to extend their reach far beyond their home market. The use of technology has enabled them to analyse customer data, create customised offers and increase customer satisfaction.

Partnerships and alliances

Some LCCs have formed partnerships with traditional airlines or other transport service providers such as bus and rail operators. These alliances allow for broader coverage and are often crucial for entering new markets.

Political stability and uniform regulations

The political stability in various European countries as well as the relative uniformity of EU regulations have made it easier for LCCs to spread across national borders. As they do not have to deal with a plethora of different national regulations, they can expand faster in a common market.

Public perception and brand identity

The image and perception of LCCs also play a role. Airlines like Ryanair and EasyJet have established themselves as reliable and low-cost options for travellers. This positive perception helps them to gain a foothold in new markets.

Cost efficiency and economies of scale

The ability of LCCs to keep their operating costs low has enabled them to offer competitive prices in new markets. As they grow in size and load factors, they benefit from economies of scale, which in turn facilitate expansion into additional markets.

Responding to the competitive landscape

Finally, LCCs have often designed their expansion in response to competitors' strategies. If a traditional airline dominates a route or market, an LCC may act as a "disruptor" and try to gain market share through lower prices or improved service.

Taken together, the expansion of LCCs in Europe is the result of a variety of factors ranging from economic and political conditions to technological developments and consumer behaviour. This complex mix of influences has enabled LCCs to offer their services beyond their home countries and profoundly change the European aviation market.

What role did EU enlargement play?

The continuous enlargement of the European Union has had a significant impact on the development and spread of LCC in Europe. This phenomenon can be viewed from different angles:

Increase the potential for market expansion

The addition of new Member States to the EU expanded the internal market, creating more opportunities for LCCs to introduce new routes and services. This was particularly the case in the new Member States in Central and Eastern Europe, where there was a strong need for low-cost travel options.

Unification of regulations and open skies agreements

EU enlargement also led to the unification of aviation regulations and standards. This standardisation made it easier for airlines to offer services across borders. Open Skies agreements, which liberalised air transport, were another important factor that allowed LCCs to include more European countries in their route networks.

Economic integration and increasing mobility

Economic integration through EU enlargement led to increased mobility of labour and capital. This increased the demand for cheap air connections for business travel and leisure. Especially for workers from the new EU countries who found work in Western European states, cheap flights became an important link to their home countries.

Incentives and subsidies

Some of the new EU Member States offered incentives and subsidies to airlines to promote their tourism sector and strengthen their economies. LCCs often took advantage of these opportunities to rapidly expand their presence in these countries.

Changing the competitive landscape

The enlargement of the EU also brought new competitors to the market, especially local LCCs from the new member states. This led to more intense competition and provided incentives for established airlines to further optimise their business models and services.

Development of consumer awareness

EU enlargement has also increased consumer awareness in the new Member States. With access to more information and options, consumers became more demanding, prompting airlines to become more responsive to customer needs.

Overall, the enlargement of the European Union had a transformative effect on LCCs and the European aviation market as a whole. It created a favourable environment for the expansion of these airlines and changed the dynamics of competition, consumer expectations and market opportunities.

Increase in cross-border services

With EU enlargement, the need for cross-border services beyond the core EU states grew. This created additional market opportunities for LCCs, especially for connections previously neglected by traditional airlines.

Unification of consumer protection rules

The EU has always sought to create uniform consumer protection standards for air passengers. These standards also apply to the new Member States, which helps LCCs to ensure a consistent service offering across the EU. At the same time, this increases consumer confidence in low-cost airline offers.

Development of the infrastructure network

The EU has made significant investments in the transport infrastructure of the new Member States, including the modernisation of airports. These investments made it more attractive for LCCs to add new destinations to the enlarged EU area.

Cultural diversity and travel trends

EU enlargement has led to greater cultural diversity. This in turn has stimulated interest in travel to lesser-known destinations, which LCCs have been able to exploit as niche operators to expand their reach.

Geopolitical considerations

The geopolitical stability fostered by EU membership can also be seen as a factor helping LCCs. Political stability is often a key criterion in the selection of new destinations and has an impact on consumer demand. For example - for obvious reasons - LCCs from Russia and Ukraine have stopped operating in the EU.

Influence on price structures and competitiveness

With the accession of new countries to the EU, LCCs also had to deal with the pricing structure and competitiveness in these markets. In some cases, they were able to benefit from lower operating costs in the new member countries.

Key moments

What events have permanently changed the industry?

Deregulation in the 1990s

Deregulation in Europe broke up the monopolies of state-owned airlines and allowed private operators to enter the market. The ability to open new routes and set prices without regulatory approval led to a rapid expansion of LCCs, which were much more innovative than the classic airlines. Companies such as Ryanair and EasyJet benefited enormously from this liberalisation and were thus able to significantly expand their route network and fleet.

Attacks of 11 September 2001

Following the attacks, security requirements for airlines worldwide were drastically increased. These new measures required significant investments in security technologies and personnel, which increased operating costs. LCCs had to find ways to minimise these additional costs, for example through improved process efficiency or increased fees for ancillary services.

Outbreak of the global financial crisis in 2008

The financial crisis had a huge impact on consumer behaviour. In a time of uncertainty and reduced spending, many consumers looked for cheaper travel options, which made LCCs gain popularity. Some even managed to increase their market share amid the economic turmoil.

Rise of the online booking platforms

Online platforms such as Skyscanner and Kayak have increased transparency in the industry as consumers can now compare prices more easily than ever before. This has led to increased competition and pressure on airlines to increase efficiency and reduce costs to remain competitive.

Environmental awareness and sustainability movements

As the focus on sustainability has grown, so have the demands on airlines to improve their carbon footprint. This has led to investments in more fuel-efficient aircraft and initiatives such as carbon offsets. In some cases, this has led LCCs to position themselves as "green" or at least "greening" alternatives.

COVID 19 pandemic

The pandemic brought international travel to a near standstill and many LCCs had to ground their fleets. This led to a number of financing and liquidity problems. However, some airlines used the crisis as an opportunity for strategic realignment, for example by adjusting their flight schedules, introducing new health and safety protocols or using their aircraft for cargo flights.

How have crises affected the industry?

Although the oil crises of the 1970s predated the LCC boom, rising fuel costs are a permanent risk for all airlines. LCCs are particularly vulnerable here as their profit margins are already low and their business models are based on extreme cost savings. When jet fuel prices rise, airlines' operating costs are increased and these costs must either be passed on to consumers or offset by cost savings elsewhere. This is where different tactics come into play:

The financial crisis of 2008 led to a recession that affected almost all sectors of the economy. In aviation, demand for air travel fell, but the impact was not entirely negative for LCCs: as both business and leisure travellers travelled less, there were fewer bookings overall. However, people who still needed or wanted to travel increasingly switched to LCC to save costs.

Some weaker or less efficient airlines went bankrupt or were taken over by stronger players, leading to a consolidation of the market. This provided new opportunities for surviving LCCs to expand.

The crisis also provided an opportunity for strategic realignment for many LCCs. Some, such as Ryanair and EasyJet, diversified their offerings and partnered with car rental companies and hotels to increase revenue.

These exemplary crises illustrate how external factors can affect the airline industry and the LCC niche in particular. They also show that amidst the challenges and turbulence there are also opportunities for growth and reorientation. Companies that are able to adapt quickly and flexibly design their business models have a better chance of surviving crises and emerging stronger than before.

Costs

Cost saving is the mantra of every LCC. However, the ways to achieve this differ. What is the composition of operating costs?

Fuel costs: The heart of the operation

The cost of jet fuel is not only high, but also volatile and influenced by a number of factors such as geopolitical developments, exchange rates and natural disasters. Some LCCs use complex hedging strategies to protect themselves against price fluctuations. They enter into contracts that fix the price of paraffin in the future so that they can plan their prices and budgets accordingly.

Personnel costs: More than just salaries

Personnel costs include not only employee salaries, but also benefits, education and training. As LCCs are focused on efficiency, they often invest in automated systems to minimise the need for labour. At the same time, salaries and working conditions often become an issue in labour disputes and negotiations with trade unions.

Airport and landing fees

LCCs tend to fly to smaller airports located outside the capital cities. These airports have the advantage that they are less busy and thus offer cheaper landing fees. However, this can also be a disadvantage for the customer, who may have to travel further distances to the desired final destination.

Maintenance and servicing

Maintenance costs can vary greatly depending on the age and condition of the aircraft fleet. New aircraft, while expensive to buy or lease, have the advantage of requiring less maintenance. To reduce maintenance costs, some LCCs also have standardised fleets, which simplifies spare parts inventory and procurement.

Marketing and Sales: Digital Strategies

In the modern era, LCCs increasingly rely on digital marketing and social media. Online booking platforms and apps reduce the need for physical ticket outlets and enable the use of dynamic pricing, which allows prices to be adjusted in real time.

Catering and on-board services

Many LCCs do not offer free meals or drinks to reduce operating costs. However, this strategy creates additional revenue streams as passengers are willing to pay for snacks, drinks or WiFi on board.

Insurance: A necessary evil

Insurance is a significant cost factor for airlines. They need to be insured against a variety of risks, including liability, property damage and business interruption.

LCCs seek to minimise these costs through a careful risk management process aimed at reducing the likelihood of insurable events.

Leasing and depreciation: A balancing act

Leasing aircraft is often less expensive than outright purchase, but comes with its own challenges, including the complexity of contracts and potential financial penalties for failures such as late returns or excessive wear and tear.

Overall, managing operating costs is a complex undertaking that requires strategic planning, constant monitoring and quick adjustments. LCCs face the particular challenge of keeping their costs down without compromising quality or safety of service.

What role does outsourcing play?

Outsourcing plays a significant role in LCC's business strategy as it is a way to reduce operating costs and focus on core operations.

Ground handling

Many LCCs prefer to outsource services such as baggage handling, check-in and boarding to specialised service companies. These companies, thanks to their specialisation and economies of scale, can often offer these services more cost-effectively than the airline itself.

Maintenance

Although maintenance is a critical aspect of an airline's safety and reliability, it is sometimes outsourced to specialised maintenance companies. These can not only offer cost efficiencies through their size and experience, but also ensure that maintenance meets international standards.

Customer service

Customer support tasks, especially related to call centres and online support, are often outsourced to external service providers. These companies have the necessary technology and training systems to provide efficient customer service, relieving the airline of the associated staff costs and infrastructure.

IT services

Information technology is another area where outsourcing comes into play. From the booking platform to the operation of internal IT systems - specialised IT service providers can often offer more efficient and cost-effective solutions.

Catering and on-board services

Some LCCs outsource the purchase and preparation of food and beverages on board to external catering companies. This allows them to save on storage and staff resources while still being able to provide an on-board offering that generates additional revenue.

Staff

Sometimes even pilots and cabin crew are recruited through specialised agencies that rely on temporary or contract labour. This allows airlines a certain flexibility, but can also generate criticism, especially with regard to working conditions and workers' rights.

Outsourcing these various functions allows LCCs to optimise their cost structure and focus on their core operations: flying passengers from one place to another at the lowest possible cost. However, outsourcing also brings challenges, particularly in terms of quality assurance, coordination with external providers and potential impact on staff working conditions. It is therefore a balancing act in which airlines must carefully consider the cost-benefit ratio.

Ultra Low Cost Carrier

Ultra-low-cost carriers (ULCCs) are a special category of low-cost airlines that extend the low-cost model to an extreme level in order to offer the lowest possible ticket prices. These airlines take cost-cutting and efficiency improvements very seriously and do everything they can to reduce operating costs to a minimum. Compared to traditional low-cost carriers (LCCs), ULCCs go one step further when it comes to lowering the base price of airline tickets while increasing the additional fees and extra costs for a range of services.

Features of ultra-low-cost carriers include:

Even greater focus on extra fees: While many low-cost carriers charge for extras such as baggage or seat selection, ULCCs are known to charge for an even wider range of services. These can even include things like printing your boarding pass at the airport or using the overhead luggage compartment.

High-density cabin configuration: ULCCs often use a very tight seating arrangement to accommodate as many passengers as possible. This means less legroom and comfort, but allows the airline to reduce the cost per passenger.

Minimalist service: On ULCCs, the on-board service is often extremely reduced. Free meals, drinks or entertainment are usually not available. Anything beyond simple transport from point A to point B is usually charged extra.

Use of secondary airports: Similar to other LCCs, ULCCs often use smaller or secondary airports to save on landing fees, although they can be even more aggressive in selecting cost-effective airports.

Fast turnaround times: ULCCs often rely on very fast turnaround times to keep the aircraft in the air as much as possible and thus generate more revenue.

Simple fare system: Fare structures are often kept very simple, with little flexibility in terms of changes or cancellations, unless the passenger pays significant fees for them.

The ULCC model certainly has its critics, mainly because of the reduced comfort and potential cost traps due to the many additional fees. However, it has also found its own niche of price-sensitive travellers who are willing to sacrifice amenities to take the cheapest flights available.

Ultra-low-cost carriers (ULCCs) also exist in Europe, with Wizz Air being a prominent example. The company is based in Hungary and offers flights to numerous destinations in Europe and beyond. Wizz Air specialises in offering extremely low-cost flights, using many of the features that distinguish ULCCs, such as fees for numerous additional services, high seat density and the use of secondary airports.

Wizz Air and similar ULCCs in Europe differ from traditional low-cost carriers such as Ryanair (the parent company of Wizz Air) and EasyJet in some respects. While Ryanair and EasyJet certainly offer low fares and charge many fees for additional services, they tend to offer a somewhat broader range of services and in some cases fly to larger airports. Ultra-low-cost carriers such as Wizz Air usually go one step further to keep operating costs as low as possible and thus offer extremely low ticket prices.

Wizz Air is also known for its rapid expansion and has even extended its flight networks to regions outside Europe, such as the Middle East. The company uses a unified fleet structure and relies on modern, fuel-efficient aircraft to maximise efficiency.

However, it is important to note that the definition of what constitutes a ULCC is not always consistent and may differ from market to market. In Europe, the aviation market as a whole is very competitive and many airlines offer a range of fares and services from very cheap to more expensive, all-inclusive options.

Overall, it can be said that the ULCC model has also gained a foothold in Europe and offers attractive options especially for price-sensitive travellers.

Sources of income

LCCs have developed a number of revenue streams beyond just ticket sales. Diversification of revenue sources is an important aspect of making these airlines' business models profitable.

Ticket sales: The main revenue generator

The sale of airline tickets remains the primary source of revenue, of course. However, LCCs have often modified the classic pricing model by offering very low base prices and then charging various surcharges for additional services.

Onboard sales

Many LCCs do not offer free meals or drinks, but sell snacks, drinks and even souvenirs during the flight. This can be a significant source of revenue as the margins for these products are often quite high.

Partnerships and cooperation

Airlines often enter into partnerships with hotels, car rental companies and travel insurance companies. By bundling these services, they can offer all-inclusive packages and in return receive a commission for each referral.

Advertising

Some LCCs use their aircraft and in-flight entertainment as advertising space. From painting the fuselage with advertising logos to ads in the in-flight magazines that passengers read during the flight, there are many ways to generate advertising revenue.

Freight and logistics services

Although the focus of LCCs is usually on passenger traffic, some also use their capacities for freight transport. This is especially the case when flights are not fully booked and there is still space for cargo.

Dynamic pricing

By using dynamic pricing algorithms, LCCs can adjust the ticket price in real time according to supply and demand. This maximises how much each seat brings in, especially during periods of high demand.

Annual or subscription models

Some LCCs are experimenting with subscription or membership models, where passengers pay an annual fee in return for access to discounted fares or exclusive offers.

Sale of customer data

Although this is a sensitive issue, airlines can also generate revenue by selling customer data to third parties. This data can be useful for market research or targeted advertising campaigns.

The main objective of these different revenue streams is to reduce dependence on the often volatile income from ticket sales. By offering a wider range of services and products, LCCs can increase their profitability while keeping the ticket price low for the consumer.

Additional fees

LCCs are known to charge a range of additional fees over and above the base fare for the flight. These fees are designed to compensate for the low ticket price and generate additional revenue. Here are some of the most common additional fees charged by LCCs:

Baggage fees

One of the most common additional charges is for checked baggage. While hand luggage is often free of charge, a separate fee is charged for checked baggage. This can vary, depending on the weight and size of the luggage, as well as when this extra service is booked.

Fees for seat selection

Many LCCs charge a fee for the ability to select a specific seat on the aircraft. This can be especially important for travellers who want more legroom or to sit next to their fellow passengers.

Priority boarding

Some airlines offer priority boarding for a fee, which allows passengers to board before other passengers. This is often attractive to those who want to make sure they can find space for their hand luggage in the overhead bins.

Change and cancellation fees

If a passenger needs to change their travel plans, there are often charges for changing the flight date, time or route. Cancellation of a flight may also incur charges and sometimes no refund is possible.

Food and drinks on board

While traditional airlines often offer free food and drinks, this is rarely the case with LCCs. Instead, passengers have the option to buy snacks and drinks on board.

Airport check-in fees

Some LCCs charge a fee when passengers check in at the airport instead of doing so online. This fee is intended to encourage online check-in and make the check-in process at the airport more efficient.

Supplementary insurance and service packages

Sometimes LCCs also offer additional insurance or service packages that include, for example, preferential treatment at baggage claim or access to airport lounges.

Fees for special baggage

Additional charges may apply for special baggage items such as sports equipment or musical instruments. These are often higher than the charges for normal checked baggage.

These additional charges contribute significantly to the profitability of LCCs, as they allow companies to keep basic costs low while still generating additional revenue. However, they are often the subject of criticism as they make it difficult to compare fares and can surprise consumers when the actual cost turns out to be significantly higher than the ticket price originally quoted

Partnerships

Airlines often partner with hotels, car rental companies and other travel service providers. When customers buy airline tickets, they are often offered the option of booking a hotel room or rental car as part of a 'travel package'. The airline receives a commission for each successful referral.

Some LCCs have credit card programmes with banks where customers can earn miles or points for every euro or dollar spent. These points can then be redeemed for future flights or other rewards.

Although less common with LCCs, there are cases where they enter into interline or codeshare agreements with other airlines. This allows passengers to seamlessly transfer from one airline to another, benefiting both partners.

The in-flight magazines, in-flight entertainment systems or even the backs of the aircraft seats can serve as advertising space. Companies pay to have their advertisements or commercials shown in these media.

LCCs use their online platforms and social media channels for advertising campaigns. These can be self-advertisements for special offers and services or include paid partnerships with other companies.

With customers' consent, airlines can send promotional emails that not only contain information on flight offers, but also advertisements for partner companies. This allows them to generate additional revenue.

Some LCCs also sell merchandise such as models of their aircraft, clothing with the company logo or other souvenirs. These items can be purchased both on board and in airport shops or online.

These partnerships and promotional activities can contribute significantly to the profitability of an LCC. Not only do they open up new revenue streams, but they also strengthen brand presence and customer loyalty, which can be crucial for business success in the long run.

Risk management

Risk management for LCCs is a complex undertaking that takes into account a variety of factors in order to make the business model sustainable and profitable. Due to thin profit margins and intense competition, effective risk management is critical for these carriers. Here are some key aspects:

The cost of aviation fuel is one of the largest items in an airline's budget. To mitigate the risk of fluctuating prices, many LCCs rely on fuel price hedging strategies, for example through the use of financial derivatives.

Some services such as aircraft maintenance, catering or customer service are often outsourced to external providers in order to save costs and focus on core operations.

Aircraft type selection and fleet maintenance are critical to minimising downtime risks and unexpected maintenance costs. Many LCCs rely on a homogeneous fleet to simplify maintenance and standardise crew training.

The risk of unprofitable routes is minimised by careful analysis of market data. Some LCCs rely on secondary airports with lower landing fees to reduce costs.

Market risks

The airline industry is highly competitive. A price war can lead to a rapid decline in margins. Good risk management therefore includes a sound pricing strategy and competitive analysis.

Demand in air travel is often seasonal. By offering special deals or diversifying target markets, LCCs try to cushion the risks from seasonality.

Changes in legislation, such as new environmental standards or taxes, can have a significant impact on operating costs. LCCs need to include these factors in their long-term planning.

Economic crises, such as the financial crisis or the COVID 19 pandemic, can have an enormous impact on demand. Effective risk management therefore includes liquidity reserves and flexible business models.

Incidents such as terrorist attacks or accidents can not only cause significant costs, but also undermine trust in the airline. Therefore, investments in security measures and crisis communication are crucial.

By effectively managing these and other risk factors, LCCs can create a stable business foundation and hedge against a variety of challenges. An integrated approach that considers financial, operational and external risks is critical for long-term success

Fuel prices

Fluctuations in fuel prices are one of the biggest challenges for all airlines, especially for LCCs that rely on low operating costs to remain profitable. As fuel represents a significant portion of an airline's operating costs, changes in fuel prices are of great importance.

Fuel price hedging (Fuel Hedging)

This is one of the most common methods of hedging against fuel price fluctuations. By buying financial derivatives, airlines set a future price for fuel. This means that the airline buys a certain amount of fuel in advance at a fixed price, regardless of whether the actual market price rises or falls. This provides a degree of price certainty and allows for better financial planning.

Fuel cost hedging, also known as "fuel hedging", is a specific financial strategy that is not covered by classic insurance policies. Instead, airlines, including LCCs, use various financial instruments and contracts to hedge against fuel price volatility. Common methods of fuel cost hedging are:

Futures and forwards

These are contracts that guarantee the purchase of a certain amount of fuel at a fixed price and time in the future. Futures are standardised contracts traded on exchanges, while forwards are negotiated individually between the parties.

Options

An option gives the airline the right, but not the obligation, to buy (call option) or sell (put option) fuel at a specific price. Options are useful when the airline wants to profit from future price fluctuations but does not want to be bound to a fixed price.

Swaps

In a swap, two parties exchange cash flows or liabilities from different financial instruments. In the context of fuel hedging, this could mean that an airline swaps a fixed price for fuel with a variable market price.

Over-the-Counter (OTC) Derivatives

These are tailor-made contracts concluded directly between the airline and a financial institution or other counterparty. They can contain very specific terms and conditions tailored to the airline's individual needs.

Efficient fleet management

LCCs tend to use modern and fuel-efficient aircraft to minimise fuel consumption per passenger kilometre. Through regular maintenance and updates, they can further improve the efficiency of their fleet.

Flexible routing and route planning

Some LCCs use algorithms and data analysis to determine the most efficient flight routes. By optimising flight routes and schedules, they can reduce fuel consumption.

Dynamic pricing

To offset the cost of fluctuations in the price of fuel, LCCs often rely on dynamic pricing. When fuel prices rise, ticket prices can be adjusted to pass on some of the additional costs to customers.

Operational adjustments

In the event of a sudden and significant increase in fuel prices, airlines may also make operational adjustments such as reducing flight frequencies on certain routes or temporarily shutting down less profitable routes.

Multi-source approach

Some airlines diversify their fuel suppliers and sources to have better negotiating potential and to hedge against local or regional price fluctuations.

By combining these different strategies, LCCs can minimise the negative impact of fuel price fluctuations and better control their operating costs. In doing so, it is crucial to constantly monitor the market situation and one's own operating data in order to be able to react quickly and efficiently to changes.

Pass-through clauses

In some cases, contracts between airlines and customers (including corporate customers and tour operators) contain clauses that allow the airline to pass on the cost of fuel fluctuations to the customer.

It is important to note that there are both opportunities and risks in using these instruments and strategies. For example, an adverse market movement can cause an airline to lose money on a hedging contract. Therefore, fuel cost hedging requires careful planning, monitoring and regular review

The Players

In Europe, there are several large LCCs that have a significant market share. These airlines have revolutionised the European airline industry and offer low-cost flights to a wide range of destinations. Here are some of the most important LCCs in Europe:

Ryanair

Based in Ireland, Ryanair is one of the largest and best-known LCCs in Europe. It serves many European countries and also offers connections to some non-European destinations. Ryanair is known for its low base fares and a variety of additional fees for extras.

EasyJet

The British company EasyJet is another important player in the European low-cost airline market. The airline offers a wide range of routes within Europe and has a particularly strong presence in the UK market.

Wizz Air

Wizz Air is a Hungarian LCC that specialises in flights in Central and Eastern Europe. However, the airline has also expanded its route network to Western European countries and now offers a number of long-haul flights. Wizz is now part of the Ryanair group

Norwegian Air Shuttle

Although Norwegian has had financial difficulties in recent years, this Norwegian LCC remains a player in Scandinavia. It was known for its low-cost transatlantic flights as well as its wide European route network. However, both are no longer offered.

Vueling

Vueling is a Spanish LCC that has an extensive route network in Southern Europe. Vueling is part of the IAG group, which also includes British Airways and Iberia.

Eurowings

As a subsidiary of the Lufthansa Group, Eurowings specializes in low-cost flights in Europe and selected long-haul flights. It is based in Germany and has several bases in Europe.

Transavia

Transavia is a Dutch LCC founded in 1965 and a subsidiary of the Air France-KLM Group. Headquartered at Amsterdam Schiphol Airport, Transavia serves a wide range of destinations in Europe and North Africa.

Laudamotion

Laudamotion, now known as Lauda and a subsidiary of Ryanair, is an Austrian LCC. Laudamotion focuses on destinations in the Mediterranean and also offers seasonal flights to various ski resorts.

Pegasus Airlines

This Turkish LCC serves domestic flights as well as numerous international destinations. It has a strong focus on the Turkish market, but is also expanding into European countries.

Jet2.com

Headquartered in the United Kingdom, Jet2.com focuses primarily on holiday destinations. The airline is known for its package travel deals that combine flights and accommodation.

TUI fly

TUI fly is part of the TUI Group and operates in various European countries, including Germany and Belgium.

The airline mainly offers flights to holiday destinations and has a strong presence in the package tour segment.

Level

Another subsidiary of the IAG Group, Level, focuses on long-haul low-cost flights, but also offers shorter European routes.

Smartwings

The Czech airline Smartwings, formerly known as Travel Service, offers scheduled flights in addition to charter flights and has expanded its presence in Europe in recent years.

AirBaltic

This Latvian airline offers a mix of low-cost and scheduled services and has a strong focus on the Baltic States, but also offers flights to many European destinations.

Volotea

The Spanish airline Volotea focuses on smaller European cities and offers direct flights that are often not served by larger airlines.

SunExpress

SunExpress is a Turkish-German joint venture and focuses on flights between Germany and Turkey, but also offers other European and intercontinental routes.

FlyPlay

This Icelandic airline mainly offers flights to and from Iceland and links them to long-haul transatlantic flights.

Most of these airlines have a specific market niche or geographical focus. Some focus on specific regions, while others try to offer a wide range of services beyond simple air travel, such as package tours or car rentals. In the wake of globalisation and thanks to the liberalisation of the European aviation market, these airlines have significantly expanded their flight networks and offer a wide range of options for travellers looking for cheap flight deals.

What distinguishes the LCC?

European LCCs have increasingly invested in greener technologies in recent years, including more fuel-efficient aircraft and biofuel options. The impact of the COVID 19 pandemic led to massive restructuring and financial challenges for many airlines. Some have even had to file for bankruptcy or have been taken over by larger groups.

The major LCCs in Europe differ in various aspects, ranging from their business model to their geographical focus and the services they offer.

Business models

Ryanair is strongly focused on cost reduction, offering extremely low base fares but with numerous additional charges.

EasyJet focuses on a balance between low cost and customer service; offers more capital and main airport routes than Ryanair.

WizzAir focuses on Central and Eastern Europe; aggressive expansion drive.

Geographical orientation

Norwegian Air Shuttle focuses on Scandinavia

Vueling focuses strongly on the Spanish and Southern European markets.

As a German airline, Eurowings has a strong presence in Germany and other German-speaking countries.

FlyPlay focuses on Iceland and transatlantic traffic.

Range of services

Jet2com Often offers package tours combining flight and accommodation.

TUI fly Specialises in seasonal flights to holiday destinations, often as part of package holidays.

Transavia has a focus on the Dutch market, but the airline also offers seasonal services to ski and beach destinations.

Market niches and specialities

Wizz Air focuses on less served markets in Central and Eastern Europe.

Volotea specialises in smaller, less frequented airports and direct connections not offered by others.

AirBaltic: In addition to its main focus on the Baltic States, the airline is also known for its investment in more environmentally friendly aircraft.

Aircraft fleet

Ryanair: Mainly uses a single aircraft type (Boeing 737-800 and new Boeing 737 max 8) to minimise maintenance costs and staff costs.

EasyJet has a relatively young Airbus fleet to maximise fuel efficiency and reliability.

FlyPlay has one of the youngest Airbus fleets in Europe.

Customer relationship and brand image

Ryanair: Often criticised for minimalist customer service, but still very successful.

EasyJet: Tries to offer a better balance between price and service and generally has a more positive image.

Vueling: Has a focus on young, tech-savvy customers and offers a user-friendly app and website.

Price structure

Ryanair: Known for their aggressive discount promotions and advertising campaigns.

Wizz Air: relies on membership programmes for loyal customers who take advantage of exclusive discounts.

Each of these airlines has its own approach to the low-cost segment, and these differences reflect the diversity of travellers they aim to serve. Although all aim to offer low-cost flights, the way they achieve this goal varies considerably.

Smaller and regional LCC

Who are the "underdogs" and niche providers?

In the European low-cost airline industry, there are several "underdogs" and niche players that have specialised in certain segments or regions and play an important role despite smaller market shares.

Laudamotion was founded by Formula 1 legend Niki Lauda and later taken over by Ryanair. The airline had specialised in holiday destinations in the Mediterranean and has since been integrated into the Ryanair brand.

Volotea: This Spanish airline specialises in connecting smaller European cities that are often ignored by the major LCCs.

AirBaltic is not a pure LCC, but it offers a range of low-cost options and specialises in the Baltic States. It is known for its investment in greener aircraft.

LEVEL: A subsidiary of IAG (International Airlines Group), LEVEL targets long-haul low-cost flights, but with a European focus on flights from Barcelona, Madrid and Paris.

SunExpress: As a Turkish-German joint venture, SunExpress focuses on flights between Germany and Turkey, but also on other European and intercontinental routes.

Eurowings Discover: A relatively new spin-off of Eurowings, specialising in holiday destinations and long-haul flights. It is an example of diversification within large aviation groups.

Niche LCC operators have the opportunity to serve particular market segments that are often overlooked or not considered lucrative enough by the major carriers. Here are some of these specialised market segments:

Regional flights and small towns

Some niche providers specialise in regional flights connecting smaller cities or remote areas. This is particularly important in geographically complex or less densely populated regions.

Ethnic or cultural connections

Some LCCs target specific ethnic or cultural groups by offering flights between countries and their diaspora communities in other countries. This could be, for example, connections between Eastern European countries and Western European cities with high migrant populations.

Business city connections

Some niche operators focus on the needs of business travellers and offer flights between important economic centres that are not served by major LCCs.

Seasonal flights

Some operators focus on seasonal markets, such as summer flights to holiday destinations or winter flights to ski resorts.

Niche holiday destinations

Some smaller LCCs specialise in lesser-known or exotic holiday destinations that are not served by the major lines.

Eco-focus

In response to growing environmental awareness, some niche operators may focus on greener flight options, such as using fuel from renewable sources or other sustainable practices.

Combined travel packages

There are providers who offer flights, accommodation and even travel experiences in a complete package. These packages are often aimed at specific target groups such as young travellers, seniors or families.

Special offers for students and young travellers

Some LCCs offer special discounts or deals for young people or students. These offers may also include flexible booking options or special connections to university cities.

Luxury cheap flights

Some niche providers try to strike a balance between low prices and a higher level of comfort to appeal to a target group that is willing to spend a little more for extra amenities.

By serving these specialised market segments, niche players in the low-cost airline industry can operate successfully and compete in an otherwise very competitive market.

Strategic alliances

Strategic alliances in aviation play a crucial role in shaping the global aviation market. These alliances allow airlines to expand their reach and services, reduce costs and better manage competition. However, the number of alliances in the low-cost sector tends to be limited to specific issues.

Global alliances

Star Alliance: The Star Alliance is one of the best-known global alliances and includes airlines such as Lufthansa, United Airlines and Singapore Airlines. Members share codeshare flights, frequent flyer programmes and airport lounges, which gives them significant cost efficiencies and enhanced reach.

Oneworld: This alliance includes airlines such as American Airlines, British Airways and Qantas. Oneworld members coordinate flight schedules and offer shared services to provide seamless travel experiences for their passengers.

SkyTeam: Delta Airlines, Air France and KLM are some of the main players in this alliance. SkyTeam aims to improve the travel experience through simplified ticket booking and check-in processes.

Codeshare agreements

Independent of global alliances, many airlines enter into codeshare agreements that allow them to operate flights under a common flight number. This extends the reach of each airline and gives passengers more flexibility in planning their journeys.

Joint ventures

Some airlines go a step further and form joint ventures to serve specific markets. This expanded partnership allows airlines to share costs and revenues on specific routes.

Strategic investments

Sometimes airlines buy shares in other airlines to consolidate a strategic partnership. This also takes place in the low-cost sector, where Ryanair has acquired several competitors (Wizz Air, Laudamotion, Mair Malta).

Specialised alliances

There are also specialised alliances for specific niches in air transport, such as cargo, maintenance or catering. These alliances can help airlines improve their services or reduce costs in specific operational areas.

Technological partnerships

The rapid development of technology has led to partnerships in the field of digitalisation and data exchange. Airlines cooperate in the development of booking systems, customer loyalty programmes or the implementation of AI and Big Data to optimise operations and improve customer service.

Response to crises

Alliances can also serve as a safety net in times of crisis, such as during the 2008 financial crisis or the COVID 19 pandemic. By sharing resources and information, airlines can better respond to unforeseen challenges.

Alliances of LCCs

The cooperations and partnerships between LCCs are often less formal and comprehensive than the large global alliances such as Star Alliance or Oneworld, which are mainly dominated by established, traditional airlines. Nevertheless, there are different types of collaborations that can be found in the low-cost airline industry:

Codeshare and interlining agreements

Some LCCs have entered into codeshare or interlining agreements to expand the route network for their passengers. These agreements allow passengers to fly multiple segments on a single ticket booking, even if operated by different airlines. An example of this was the partnership between EasyJet and Norwegian Air on certain European routes.

Joint purchasing strategies

To achieve cost efficiencies, sometimes several LCCs join forces for joint purchases, for example of aircraft or fuel. By purchasing together, they can negotiate volume discounts and better contract terms.

Business cooperation

Some LCCs also share resources such as maintenance facilities, crew training centres or ground handling services. This type of cooperation helps to keep operating costs low.

Franchise and licensing models

There are cases where an established LCC licenses its brand and business model to smaller or start-up airlines. This allows the new airline to quickly establish a market presence while the established airline expands its route network without having to invest new resources itself.

Marketing and advertising partnerships

Joint marketing initiatives, such as coordinated advertising campaigns or sponsorship deals, may also exist between LCCs. These partnerships are often limited in time and aim to promote special offers or new routes.

Digital platforms and booking systems

Digitalisation has made it easier to establish partnerships in booking and customer service infrastructure. Some LCCs integrate their booking systems to enable cross-selling and a seamless customer experience.

Strategic participations

Although less common, there are cases where one LCC invests in another to gain strategic advantages, such as better market access or cooperation in specific business areas.

Although these cooperations are often less formalised than the alliances of traditional airlines, they nevertheless enable LCCs to optimise their operating costs, expand their market presence and diversify their services. They represent a flexible and pragmatic approach to partnerships in a highly competitive market environment.

Through cooperation, airlines can reduce their operating costs. This is particularly important for LCCs, where cost efficiency is crucial. Joint purchases, shared services and operating resources contribute to this.

Partnerships and alliances expand an airline's route network without large investments in new aircraft or infrastructure. Codesharing and interlining allow airlines to offer more destinations, which is attractive to customers.

In a volatile market, alliances can serve as a buffer. Joint risk management strategies, such as fuel price hedges, can increase financial stability. Alliances can facilitate entry into new markets, as established partners can share their expertise and market knowledge. This is particularly helpful in the case of regulatory hurdles or cultural differences.

By sharing frequent flyer programmes and other customer loyalty initiatives, airlines can expand and consolidate their customer base. By sharing resources such as maintenance facilities or training centres, airlines can increase their operational efficiency.

Managing an alliance can be complex, especially if it involves many partners or very different business models. This can lead to inefficient processes or communication difficulties. Alliances and partnerships can raise competition concerns, especially if they promote a dominant market position.

When an airline shares its brand and services with another airline through an alliance, it cedes some control over quality and the customer experience.

In financially unstable times, the risks of one partner can have an impact on the other alliance members. This is especially true if there are financial obligations or close operational linkages.

The goals and strategies of the alliance partners may not always be fully aligned, which can lead to conflicts. For example, different growth objectives or business philosophies could affect the effectiveness of the alliance. Problems at one alliance partner, such as security concerns or poor customer service, can damage the reputation of the entire alliance and its members.

It should be noted that alliances are much less common in the LCC sector than in traditional aviation.

Regulations and legislation

Aviation is a highly regulated sector governed by a multitude of laws and regulations at local, national and international levels. These regulations cover various aspects, from aviation safety to environmental protection.

Flight safety

ICAO (International Civil Aviation Organisation): This UN agency sets international standards for civil aviation, including safety guidelines.

FAA (Federal Aviation Administration) and EASA (European Aviation Safety Agency): These organisations are responsible for regulating aviation in the US and EU respectively. They ensure that aircraft, crews and airlines are safety compliant.

National authorities: In many countries, there are additional national agencies that regulate local aviation.

Environmental protection

Emissions trading and CO2 pricing: In the EU, aviation is integrated into the Emissions Trading Scheme (EU ETS), which prices CO2 emissions.

Noise regulation: Airports and airlines must comply with certain noise standards.

Consumer protection

Air passenger rights: There are extensive regulations in the EU to protect air passengers, known as EU Regulation 261/2004, which sets out what compensation is payable in the event of delays, cancellations and overbooking.

Transparency in pricing: Airlines are often required by competition law to transparently display all fees and surcharges in the ticket price.

Market access and competition

Open Skies Agreement

The concept of "open skies" refers to air transport agreements that aim to liberalise the air transport market by reducing or eliminating restrictions on the choice of routes, the number of flights and fares. In the European Union, the European Common Aviation Area provides the basis for a liberalised market that allows airlines to operate within Member States without major restrictions. This is in line with the general objectives of the internal market, which promotes the free movement of persons, goods, services and capital.

The EU-US Open Skies Agreement, which came into force in 2007, is one of the best-known examples. It allows European and American airlines to fly between any point in the European Union and any point in the United States. Before this agreement, transatlantic flights were governed by bilateral agreements between individual European countries and the US, which were often restrictive and gave certain airlines exclusive rights to certain routes. The Open Skies agreement broke up these monopolies and promoted competition, usually resulting in lower prices and more choice for consumers.

The European Union has also concluded similar agreements with a number of other countries and regions, including Canada, certain countries in Asia and Africa, and several countries neighbouring the EU. These agreements vary in scope and complexity, but all aim to liberalise the aviation market and promote competition.

Restrictions of competition

Many countries have restrictions on foreign ownership of domestic airlines.

Airlines are also subject to general competition laws that prohibit cartels and other anti-competitive practices.

Labour law

Flight crews and ground staff are subject to both national and international labour laws governing working hours, rest periods, pay and other working conditions.

Security and surveillance

Airlines also have to implement a number of security procedures, including strict passenger and baggage screening, which are regulated by national and international authorities.

In the EU, many of these aspects are harmonised through EU law and cooperation between member states. However, national differences may exist in the implementation and interpretation of the laws. It is a complex web of regulations that is constantly updated to respond to new challenges and developments in the aviation sector.

EU law

EU legislation has a significant impact on the airline industry in Europe, especially on LCCs.

Market liberalisation and competition

The EU has opened up the aviation market through a series of liberalisation measures that allow airlines to operate within the EU without major restrictions. This has led to LCCs such as Ryanair and EasyJet expanding rapidly and entering new markets.

Air passenger rights

With EU Regulation 261/2004, the EU has introduced strict rules on passenger compensation for delays, cancellations and overbooking. This has increased operating costs for airlines, but also strengthened consumer protection.

Environmental protection

The inclusion of aviation in the European Emissions Trading Scheme (EU ETS) has led to airlines having to pay for their $CO2$ emissions. This encourages the development and implementation of greener technologies.

Safety standards

The European Aviation Safety Agency (EASA) plays a central role in setting safety standards in European aviation. Its requirements must be met by all airlines operating in the EU, which is particularly relevant for LCCs that want to keep their costs down.

Labour law and social standards

EU regulations also set minimum standards for the working conditions of flight staff. This concerns aspects such as maximum working hours, rest periods and safety training. These regulations influence the personnel policy and thus also the cost structure of LCCs.

Data protection

With the introduction of the General Data Protection Regulation (GDPR), airlines must comply with strict data protection measures, especially with regard to the storage and processing of passenger data.

Additional fees and transparency

The EU values transparency in pricing and has therefore issued rules requiring airlines to disclose all additional charges and surcharges in advance.

Slot regulation

The allocation of take-off and landing times at airports, known as "slots", is also regulated by the EU. Slot management can be particularly problematic for LCCs, which often want to fly at unusual times to save costs. The EU has implemented mechanisms to ensure a fair distribution of slots, but this remains a controversial issue.

Cabotage rights

Within the EU, airlines from member states are allowed to operate cabotage flights, i.e. flights that take off and land within a foreign country. This regulation allows LCCs to enter new domestic markets in other EU countries.

Geoblocking

The EU has banned geo-blocking measures, which means that airlines cannot charge EU citizens different prices based on their nationality or place of residence. This has particularly affected online booking platforms.

Brexit and its effects

The UK's exit from the EU had significant consequences for the aviation industry. Airlines with strong links to the UK, such as Ryanair and EasyJet, have had to adapt their operational structures to remain compliant with EU regulations. EasyJet, for example, has flagged out part of its fleet to Austria.

Taxes and duties

The EU also has an influence on the taxation of air travel. Although tax legislation is mainly in the hands of the member states, there are EU-wide minimum standards for air traffic taxes, VAT and similar levies that all airlines must take into account.

Future regulations

It is also important to keep an eye on the future direction of EU legislation. Issues such as sustainable aviation and the integration of drones into the airspace are likely to become an increasing focus of EU regulation.

Failure to comply with EU legislation can lead to significant penalties and litigation. This represents a financial and operational risk for airlines, which must always be vigilant to comply with all legal requirements.

So while EU legislation creates opportunities for LCCs through market liberalisation and cabotage rights, it also presents them with significant challenges in areas such as consumer protection, environmental regulation and compliance. An airline's ability to adapt to these complex and ever-changing regulations can be crucial to its long-term success.

Safety standards

Aviation safety rules are extremely strict and are monitored and enforced by a variety of organisations at international, regional and national levels. In the European context, the European Aviation Safety Agency (EASA) plays a crucial role in setting safety standards. Here are some of the main areas where safety rules apply:

Aircraft certification

Before an aircraft type is allowed to enter service, it must undergo a series of rigorous tests and certifications. These include structural tests, system tests and performance evaluations.

Operating procedure

Airlines must adhere to strict operating procedures, ranging from aircraft maintenance to navigation processes. For example, pilots must go through certain checklists before the flight takes off and after it lands.

Crew training

Pilots, co-pilots and flight attendants must undergo extensive training and regular further training. This includes both theory and practical exercises, including the use of flight simulators.

Air traffic management

Air traffic control systems are responsible for managing the safe flow of aircraft in the sky and at airports. This includes monitoring the airspace and providing information and instructions to pilots.

Airport security

This includes both the physical security of the infrastructure and the monitoring of passengers and baggage. This includes security checks, surveillance cameras and special security procedures for cargo traffic.

Communication

Reliable communication channels between the cockpit, air traffic control and ground personnel are crucial for flight safety. Specialised frequencies and communication systems are used for this purpose.

Emergency plans

Airlines are required to have comprehensive contingency plans that take effect in cases such as hijacking, technical failures or extreme weather conditions. Staff are regularly trained in the implementation of these plans.

Monitoring and audits

Compliance with safety rules is monitored through regular inspections and audits by external and internal organisations. Violations can lead to penalties, operating restrictions or, in the worst case, withdrawal of the operating licence.

As aviation is an international industry by nature, there are also a number of international agreements and organisations that promote aviation safety, including the International Civil Aviation Organization (ICAO).

Overall, compliance with safety rules forms the basis for the operations of every player in the aviation industry. The rules are complex and multi-layered and require a continuous effort from all stakeholders to ensure the highest safety standards.

Differences to traditional airlines

In terms of safety standards, there are basically no differences between LCC and traditional airlines, as both types of airlines are subject to the same regulatory requirements. The European Aviation Safety Agency (EASA) and similar organisations in other regions set strict safety guidelines that must be followed by all airlines, regardless of whether they are low-cost or premium. These requirements cover aircraft maintenance, pilot training, operations and numerous other aspects of aviation safety.

However, there are a few areas where the practices of LCCs and traditional airlines might differ:

Operating models

LCCs often operate a point-to-point model, avoiding complex hub-and-spoke networks used by many traditional airlines. This simpler operating model can reduce the risk of delays and the associated risk of safety issues caused by overloaded crews or maintenance teams.

Turnaround times

LCCs often strive for fast turnaround times to maximise profitability. Although this improves efficiency, it could theoretically lead to concerns about aircraft maintenance and inspection. However, these fast turnarounds must not compromise safety compliance.

Crew resources

Some LCCs are trying to reduce costs by having fewer cabin crew on board, but still remain within regulatory requirements. While the number of cabin crew remains within regulations, this could have an impact on the ability to evacuate passengers in the event of an emergency.

Use of older aircraft

Some LCCs use older aircraft models to save costs. Although these aircraft must undergo the same maintenance and safety checks as newer models, they may have less modern safety features.

Economic considerations

LCCs are strongly focused on keeping operating costs low. However, there are clear regulations that ensure that economic considerations must not compromise safety.

Safety record of low-cost airlines?

The safety record of LCCs is generally similar to that of traditional airlines. As all airlines, whether LCC or not, are subject to the same safety regulations and controls, there are no systematic differences in safety between the two types of airlines. Monitoring by regulators such as the European Aviation Safety Agency (EASA) and national aviation authorities ensures that all airlines comply with strict safety standards.

Factors influencing the safety record

Age of the fleet: Newer aircraft often have more modern security systems, which can increase safety. Some LCCs, such as Ryanair, operate very modern fleets that meet the highest safety standards.

Maintenance: Regardless of the business model, all airlines must comply with the same maintenance requirements. Poor maintenance can lead to safety issues, but there is no evidence that LCCs perform worse in this area.

Pilot training: Pilots at LCC undergo the same basic training as pilots at traditional airlines, and they must pass similar exams and certifications.

Corporate culture: In some cases, the corporate culture that focuses on safety could have an impact on the safety record. However, this is difficult to quantify and varies from company to company.

Statistical data

Although it is difficult to make direct comparisons, statistical data shows that commercial aviation is generally safe. There are very few accidents and the vast majority of flights occur without incident. Accidents that do occur are thoroughly investigated to prevent future incidents, regardless of whether it is an LCC or a traditional airline.

In 2022, there were around 115 accidents involving aircraft with more than 12 seats in Europe (not only the EU), of which - depending on the definition - only around four involved so-called low-cost carriers. No one was injured in these mainly minor incidents. An example is the carrier Ryanair, which had no accidents at all in 2022.

Media coverage

Sometimes media coverage can influence the public perception of LCC safety. A single incident can receive excessive attention, leading to a distorted perception of the overall safety record.

By and large, the safety record of LCCs in Europe is extremely robust and there are no significant systematic differences in safety between LCCs and traditional airlines. Both types of airlines are highly regulated and must adhere to strict safety standards.

Environmental laws

The airline industry is subject to a number of environmental regulatory requirements aimed at minimising the sector's environmental footprint. These requirements apply to both LCCs and traditional airlines and are set by various regulatory bodies at national and international level.

Emission standards

Airlines must meet specific emission standards set by organisations such as the International Civil Aviation Organization (ICAO). These standards regulate the emission of greenhouse gases and other pollutants such as nitrogen oxides.

Noise regulations

There are also noise regulations that limit the permissible decibel levels of aircraft during take-off, flight and landing. These are usually set by national aviation authorities in cooperation with international organisations.

Flight routes and airspace use

Optimising flight routes and airspace use is also seen as a way to reduce fuel consumption and thus CO_2 emissions. Air traffic control centres and airlines often work together to plan more efficient flight routes.

CO_2 compensation and emissions trading

In the European Union, airlines must participate in the Emissions Trading Scheme (ETS), which provides a market for CO_2 emission allowances. Airlines that emit more CO_2 than allowed must buy emission allowances from other companies that are below their emission targets.

Renewable energies and sustainable fuels

The use of sustainable aviation fuels and research into alternative propulsion methods are other areas in which airlines are active to reduce their environmental impact.

Waste management

Many airlines have implemented programmes to reduce waste generated on board and promote recycling.

Although this is less directly regulated, there are best practices and sometimes regulations at national level that address waste disposal and recycling.

Finally, there are requirements to disclose environmental information. Airlines are generally required to report publicly on their CO_2 emissions and other environmental impacts. It is important to note that non-compliance with these requirements can lead to heavy fines, operating restrictions or, in extreme cases, revocation of the operating licence. Therefore, environmental compliance is a critical aspect of any airline's operations.

How is the airlines' carbon footprint regulated?

The regulation of airlines' carbon footprint is a complex system made up of international agreements, European and national regulations, and internal industry initiatives. Here are some of the main aspects of CO_2 regulation in the aviation industry:

International agreements

The International Civil Aviation Organization (ICAO) is the UN agency responsible for regulating the global aviation industry. ICAO has established the Carbon Offsetting and Reduction Scheme for International Aviation (CORSIA), which aims to limit the growth of CO_2 emissions from international civil aviation.

EU Emissions Trading Scheme (ETS)

Within the European Union, airlines operating in EU countries must participate in the Emissions Trading Scheme (ETS). This system sets a cap on the amount of CO_2 emissions that airlines can emit. Companies that exceed their emissions targets must buy emissions allowances, while those that fall short of their targets can sell their surplus allowances.

National regulations

Some countries have introduced their own mechanisms to regulate airlines' CO_2 emissions. These can include taxes, fees or specific emission reduction targets.

Industry initiatives

In addition to legal requirements, there are also internal industry efforts to reduce CO_2 emissions. These can include promoting research and development into sustainable fuels, introducing more efficient aircraft models or operational changes to reduce fuel consumption.

Transparency and reporting

Airlines are usually required to report on their CO_2 emissions and progress in reducing them. These reports can be verified by independent auditing organisations and made public, providing both regulators and the public with insight into the airlines' carbon footprint.

Sanctions and incentives

Non-compliance with CO2 regulations can lead to a range of sanctions, including fines and operating restrictions. At the same time, there are also incentives such as subsidies or tax benefits for companies that proactively take measures to reduce their CO2 emissions.

Regulation of airlines' carbon footprint is a constantly evolving field, especially given the growing importance of climate change. It is expected that regulations will be further tightened in the coming years in order to meet the goals of the Paris Agreement and other global climate targets.

Competition and market dynamics

Price wars

Price wars between LCCs are a well-known phenomenon and a characteristic feature of this business segment. In their constant search for competitive advantage and market share, LCCs often use aggressive pricing strategies to attract customers. This occasionally leads to so-called "price wars" in which airlines massively lower their prices in order to compete against the competition.

In times of high demand (e.g. holiday periods), prices are generally higher, but in the low season or at less busy times, airlines may lower their prices to fill seats and hurt competition.

When an airline lowers its prices, competitors often react by reducing prices to remain competitive. This can lead to a domino effect.

Many LCCs use algorithms that adjust ticket prices in real time based on factors such as load factor, booking time and market demand. These do not always work in the same way and can thus also have uncalculated effects.

In the short term, consumers benefit from the low prices and have the opportunity to travel at very favourable conditions.

In the long term, price wars can affect the profitability of the airlines involved. This can lead to financial difficulties and, in the worst case, insolvency.

The aggressive pricing policy can also mean that the quality of service suffers, as airlines have to make savings elsewhere to compensate for the low prices.

Another critical aspect is the question of how such price wars are compatible with sustainability goals. Extremely low ticket prices could make flying even more attractive and thus increase CO_2 emissions, which is in direct contradiction to global and European climate goals.

Price wars in aviation, especially among LCCs, have a number of significant implications for the industry:

Price cuts often lead to an immediate increase in ticket bookings. This can be beneficial for airlines looking to fill seats quickly, especially in low seasons or on less popular routes.

Aggressive pricing strategies, however, can weigh heavily on profit margins. This is particularly problematic for smaller or less financially stable airlines that do not have the same resources as larger competitors.

Prolonged price wars may lead to industry consolidation, with only the most competitive companies surviving. This could reduce competition in the medium to long term.

To keep costs down, airlines may try to reduce labour costs, which can lead to poorer working conditions for staff.

Consistently low price levels can lead to consumers starting to see low prices as the norm, which increases the pressure on airlines to continue to keep their costs low.

In an effort to keep costs as low as possible, airlines may reduce the quality of customer service and in-flight amenities.

Long-term price wars could damage the general reputation of the industry if consumers start to question the safety and reliability of LCC, even if there is no objective reason for this.

Price wars could make flying accessible to more people and thus increase energy consumption and CO_2 emissions, with negative effects on the environment.

Incentivising more frequent flying through lower prices is at odds with global and especially European targets to reduce greenhouse gas emissions.

In summary, price wars lead to a complex mix of benefits and challenges for the airline industry. They are an indicator of intense competition, but can also threaten the financial stability of companies and the quality of service, and have potentially negative impacts on the environment and the sustainability of the industry.

Mergers and acquisitions

Acquisitions and mergers are an important feature of the airline industry, and LCCs are no exception. They are a means of expansion and can also be a survival strategy for companies in a highly competitive market. Here are some notable acquisitions and mergers that have taken place between European LCCs in the past:

Ryanair and Buzz

In 2003, the Irish low-cost airline Ryanair took over the Dutch airline Buzz from KLM. With the takeover, Ryanair expanded to several European routes and strengthened its position in the market.

EasyJet and Go Fly

The acquisition of Go Fly by EasyJet in 2002 was a key moment for the industry. The merger made EasyJet one of the largest LCCs in Europe.

Air Berlin and dba

In 2006, the German airline Air Berlin took over the also German airline dba (formerly Deutsche BA). This takeover was an attempt by Air Berlin to strengthen its domestic network. However, Air Berlin later went bankrupt and was partially taken over by Lufthansa and EasyJet in 2017.

Norwegian and FlyNordic

The Norwegian LCC Norwegian Air Shuttle took over the Swedish airline FlyNordic in 2007, thus expanding its presence in the Scandinavian region.

Vueling and Clickair

In 2009, the Spanish LCCs Vueling and Clickair merged, creating one of the largest LCCs in Spain. Iberia, the parent company of Clickair, received a minority stake in Vueling as part of the merger.

Wizz Air and Wizz Air Ukraine

Wizz Air, one of the largest low-cost airlines in Eastern Europe, decided in 2015 to close its Ukrainian subsidiary Wizz Air Ukraine and integrate its operations into the main airline. This was a strategic decision responding to the political and economic instability in Ukraine.

Other takeovers, for example by Ryanair (Wizz Air, Laudamotion, Air Malta) have already been discussed elsewhere.

These acquisitions and mergers show that European LCCs are in a constant state of change and adaptation. They are actively looking for ways to expand and improve their competitive position, and acquisitions are one of the ways they do this.

Mergers and acquisitions between LCCs can have significant effects on competition in the airline industry. The effects can be manifold, with both positive and negative consequences for different stakeholders.

Strengthening market position: Through mergers, airlines can consolidate their market position and better hold their own against the competition. The additional capital and resources can be used for expansion, technology improvements and other strategic investments.

Synergy effects: Merged companies can benefit from synergies in the form of improved operations, a more comprehensive network and lower costs through economies of scale.

Cost efficiency: Mergers can lead to cost reductions as redundant functions can be eliminated and efficiencies in operational processes can be achieved.

Reduced competition: One of the main disadvantages is that mergers can reduce competition in the market. When two large low-cost airlines merge, the number of players in the market is reduced, which could limit consumer choice and raise prices.

Barriers to market entry: Mergers can make it more difficult for new or smaller players to enter or compete in the market, as merged firms have stronger market power.

Job loss: The cost efficiencies achieved through mergers often lead to job losses as companies seek to eliminate duplicate roles and reduce operating costs.

Quality degradation: In a less competitive market, merged firms may have less incentive to improve or maintain the quality of their services and products.

It is also important to note that mergers and acquisitions are usually reviewed by competition authorities for their impact on the market. These reviews may impose conditions on the merger or even block it if it is found that it would significantly impede competition.

Booking platforms or apps?

Online bookings play a crucial role in the LCC business model and in the modern travel market as a whole.

Booking platforms

Platforms such as Skyscanner, Kayak, Fluege.de and Momondo and many others aggregate flight offers from various airlines, including LCCs, and then redirect the user to the airline's or a third-party provider's website. Through this listing on meta-search engines or other booking platforms, LCCs increase their visibility and reach a wider audience.

LCCs save marketing costs if they are listed on popular booking platforms, as the platforms themselves place advertisements to generate traffic. However, booking platforms usually take a commission for each booking made through their platform, which reduces the LCC's profit margins.

By listing on a booking platform, the airline brand might fade into the background as the focus is on comparing ticket prices. For consumers, booking platforms are convenient as they can compare multiple offers on a single page. However, sometimes consumers may also incur additional fees that are not visible at first glance, making it difficult to compare prices.

Many platforms offer additional services such as hotel bookings, car rental and travel insurance, often in package deals that provide additional revenue streams for both the platform and the airline.

Apps

LCC apps, on the other hand, only offer the option of booking with a single airline. However, they also offer many other options such as online check-in, seat selection, boarding passes and much more. It is therefore no wonder that almost all low-cost airlines today have their own booking apps and at the same time prohibit the distribution of their flights via booking apps or third-party websites.

Flexibility in booking

LCCs are known for their strict cancellation policies. However, some offer some flexibility in rebooking or cancellation for an extra charge.

Many LCCs offer an à la carte structure for additional services such as seat selection, extra baggage or priority boarding. Customers can use this flexibility to tailor their flight to their needs.

Some LCCs and booking platforms allow more complex bookings, such as open-jaw flights (outbound and return from different airports) or flights with multiple stopovers. However, this is only the exception to the rule, which applies more to established airlines.

Payment options and flexibility in booking are key factors influencing the customer experience when using LCC. They can also be important decision criteria when consumers choose between different providers. While LCCs typically offer less flexibility than traditional carriers, many try to remain competitive by offering a variety of payment options and certain customisation options.

In-flight experience

The in-flight experience at LCCs is usually quite different from that at traditional airlines, mainly because of the business model, which aims to keep costs as low as possible.

LCCs tend to reduce seat pitch to accommodate more passengers and thus reduce the cost per seat.

Many LCCs offer seat selection only for an additional fee. If you don't want to pay an extra fee, the seat is often assigned randomly.

Unlike many traditional airlines, LCCs almost always charge for in-flight catering. The offer ranges from snacks and drinks to simple meals.

Alcoholic drinks are also chargeable and prices can be comparatively high.

In-flight entertainment systems are rarely found in LCCs, and when they are, it is often for a fee. If Wi-Fi is available, it is often chargeable and the connection can be slow or unreliable.

Upgrade options: Some LCCs offer upgrades that include additional comfort or benefits such as priority boarding, but at an additional cost.

Customer interaction and service

Many services, such as check-in and baggage check-in, are self-service, which reduces the need for staff and thus costs.

Flight attendants tend to be focused on safety aspects and selling products and services, rather than comprehensive customer service.

LCCs have clearly placed their focus on cost efficiency, which is reflected in the limited in-flight experience. Nevertheless, many of these airlines seek to generate additional revenue streams through optional fees and upgrades, while providing an acceptable experience for passengers.

Quality of in-flight catering and other services

The quality of in-flight catering and other services on LCCs can vary widely, but generally depends on the aim to keep operating costs as low as possible. The choice of food and beverages is often limited and usually only snacks and simple meals are offered. As catering is almost always chargeable, passengers often try to avoid this expense, which leads to less demand and therefore less variety in the offer. As costs have to be saved, LCCs tend to rely on products with a long shelf life rather than fresh produce.

The quality of baggage service can vary, but LCCs tend to have strict baggage policies with high charges for excess baggage.

While some LCCs are known for their punctuality, this is not always the case. As these airlines often operate their planes at full capacity and have fast turnaround times, delays can occur relatively quickly.

Overall, the quality of service on LCCs is usually not comparable to that on traditional airlines. However, it offers an acceptable standard for passengers who are willing to make sacrifices in comfort in order to save money.

Before the flight

Customer service and booking: Many LCCs operate a lean call centre and rely on online bookings. A well-designed online booking system and efficient customer service can facilitate the booking process and leave a positive first impression. Service in the traditional sense is usually not to be expected here - or only at a high surcharge.

As LCCs often have strict baggage policies, counter staff are responsible for communicating these rules effectively and clearly.

Boarding process: Airlines use a variety of boarding methods, and the efficiency and friendliness of ground staff can weigh heavily in this. Some LCCs offer priority boarding as a chargeable service. The boarding process is sometimes more reminiscent of a bus journey than an air journey.

Customer reviews

Online reviews play an increasingly important role for LCC's business in today's digital world, as they can strongly influence the public perception of a brand. They are an important source of information for potential customers and can have both positive and negative effects.

Good reviews can strengthen trust in the airline and attract new customers. Positive reviews and high rating numbers can help an airline rank higher in the search results of booking and comparison portals. Satisfied customers often share their positive experiences on social networks, which acts as free advertising for the airline. With a high rating average, airlines may be able to justify higher prices, as customers are more willing to pay for a service they perceive to be of high quality.

Negative reviews can seriously damage an airline's reputation, especially if these reviews attract viral attention.

A poor online reputation can lead to a decrease in bookings and therefore lost revenue. Negative reviews can lead to the airline having to invest in damage limitation, be it through PR campaigns, customer service or even litigation.

Airlines, especially LCCs, must therefore actively develop strategies to manage their online reputation. This can include monitoring review platforms, building an efficient customer service to respond to complaints and questions, and regularly updating information and services. Some airlines also use specialised software to monitor and analyse online reviews to identify trends and take proactive action.

Social media and influencers

Social media and influencers are playing an increasingly important role in the aviation industry, especially for LCCs looking to increase their reach and visibility without large marketing budgets.

Through platforms such as Facebook, Twitter and Instagram, LCCs can communicate directly with their target group. They not only provide information about offers and services, but also use these platforms to build a brand image.

Real-time customer service: Social media allows airlines to respond in real time to customer complaints or requests, which can increase customer satisfaction.

In case of delays, strikes or other unforeseen events, social media channels provide a platform for quick and transparent communication. Through social listening, airlines can better understand and respond to trends and customer needs. Influencers offer a kind of "word-of-mouth propaganda 2.0". Their recommendations appear more authentic than classic advertising and can thus create a higher level of credibility and trust. Influencers often have a very specific following, which makes it easier for LCC to target a specific audience. High-quality content from influencers can be reused for marketing purposes. This saves airlines time and resources in content creation. A successful influencer campaign can attract viral attention, significantly increasing the airline's reach and awareness.

Economic and social impacts of LCC

Tourism

LCCs have made it possible for a wider section of the population to travel. Low ticket prices boost tourism in many areas that were previously less visited. The increased flow of tourists generates more revenue for local shops, hotels and service providers, which boosts the local economy. LCC's low prices also force traditional airlines and other modes of transport such as rail and bus to adjust their pricing structures, which further boosts tourism.

LCCs make travel accessible to people who could not afford it before, thus promoting a certain "democratisation of travel". The possibility to travel cheaply has also changed travel habits. Short trips and weekend getaways are becoming more popular, which also leads to a shift in the type of tourism offers.

However, the increase in air travel by LCC also has negative environmental impacts, especially in terms of CO_2 emissions and global warming.

The increase in tourism can in some cases lead to an overload of local infrastructures and natural resources.

Increased mobility promotes cultural exchange, but can also lead to the "McDonaldisation" of tourist destinations, displacing local cultures and traditions.

The increased demand in the tourism sector due to LCC creates jobs in various sectors such as the hotel industry, gastronomy and the service industry. Although more jobs are created, these are often seasonal and sometimes low-paid, which can affect the social structure in the destinations.

Many LCCs use smaller or secondary airports, often far from the city centre. This can present both advantages and challenges for the local transport infrastructure.

Increased tourism activity can lead to overloading of local infrastructures, which in turn requires investment in sustainable development projects.

The low-cost airline culture promotes "fast tourism", where travellers go on more frequent but shorter trips. This has implications for the way tourism is consumed and experienced.

The mass arrival of tourists can lead to a loss of authenticity, as local customs and cultures can be influenced by "mainstream" tourism.

Impact on local economies and tourism industry

Economic upswing through tourism

LCCs make it possible for a wide range of people to travel. This leads to increased tourist activity, which revitalises local shops, hotels and restaurants in the destination regions. This increase in economic activity can boost the local economy and contribute to the prosperity of the region.

Rising land prices and cost of living

However, the increased tourist activity and the accompanying economic boom can also have negative effects. In some cases, land prices and the cost of living for the local population are rising, which can lead to displacement effects and social tensions.

Seasonality and jobs

Tourism is often a seasonal industry. This means that while jobs are created, they are often seasonal and offer little long-term job security. Moreover, these jobs can often be low-paid and offer no additional social benefits.

Fiscal revenue and investment in infrastructure

The increase in travel activities leads to increased revenues from tourism taxes and other levies. These funds can in turn be invested in local infrastructure, such as the expansion of transport networks or the improvement of education and health systems.

Displacement of traditional industries

In some cases, tourism, fuelled by LCC, can displace traditional local industries. If resources are increasingly turned to the tourism sector, other economic activities may suffer.

Environmental impact and sustainable development

Increased tourist activity can also put pressure on the environment, especially in areas known for their natural richness and beauty. This raises sustainable development issues and requires careful planning and regulation.

Working conditions in the industry

Employment models and workers' rights

Working conditions and workers' rights at LCC are a controversial and much-discussed topic, which is often viewed critically by the public. In the following I will explain some aspects that are relevant in this context.

Employment contracts and employment status

In many cases, LCCs use atypical employment models such as fixed-term contracts, part-time work or agency work. These models can offer workers less security and less access to social benefits. In some cases, flight attendants and pilots are classified as self-employed, making it difficult for them to obtain protection from labour rights and trade unions.

Wages and social benefits

Wages are often lower than traditional airlines and there may be fewer benefits. However, some LCCs offer performance-based incentives such as bonuses or revenue sharing that can supplement salary.

Working hours and rest periods

Working hours can be long and irregular, often with short rest periods between shifts. This can lead to exhaustion and stress, which can affect not only workers' health but also flight safety.

Trade union representation

Union representation can be weaker at LCCs than at established airlines. Some LCCs have tried to prevent the formation of unions or to replace independent unions with company-owned employee representation.

Health and safety

Although LCCs in the EU are subject to the same safety standards as other airlines, working conditions, especially long hours and stress, can have health effects on employees.

Legal framework

Working conditions and workers' rights are regulated by a number of directives and regulations in the European Union. However, the implementation of these laws is monitored by member states and there may be differences in application and enforcement. Furthermore, since Brexit, working conditions in the UK may differ from those in the EU.

Training and qualification opportunities

While some LCCs invest in staff training, this is not always the rule. Often, employees are expected to already be fully qualified and little to no training is required. This can limit employees' professional development and lead to higher turnover.

Geographical mobility

In LCC, geographical mobility of staff is often a requirement. Many employees must be willing to work in different locations, which can lead to a lack of job security and stability.

Discrimination and diversity

There have been reports of discrimination based on gender, nationality or age in the low-cost airline industry. This raises questions about compliance with equality directives and other labour law provisions.

Psychological factors

Working conditions, especially stress and long working hours, can also have psychological effects. This can lead to burnout, depression and other mental health problems that are often inadequately addressed.

Job security

Due to the price-sensitive business model of LCCs, job security is often less guaranteed than with traditional airlines. Especially in difficult economic times or price wars, this can lead to mass layoffs or the closure of locations.

There is a growing movement of workers' organisations, political actors and the public demanding improvement of working conditions. Some LCCs have already taken action to change their practices, but there is still much room for improvement.

As the low-cost airline industry continues to grow, so does the pressure to improve working conditions.

Whether this will be through government regulation, trade union activity or by the companies themselves remains to be seen.

Overall, these complementary points show that working conditions and workers' rights at LCCs are a complex and multi-layered issue that encompasses many challenges and criticisms. The debate on this is ongoing and it is likely that we will see further changes and adjustments in the coming years.

Ethics and criticism

Discussion about environmentally harmful practices

The discussion about environmentally harmful practices at LCCs has become louder and louder in recent years. In view of global climate change and the increasing urgency to reduce CO_2 emissions, LCCs in particular have come under criticism for making flying accessible to broad sections of the population and thus increasing air traffic overall.

Public perception

LCCs are often portrayed as a symbol of irresponsible fossil fuel use. Their business models, based on high utilisation and fast turnaround times, are seen as counter-productive in the effort to reduce global CO_2 emissions.

Policy measures

Various policy instruments, such as an aviation tax based on CO_2 emissions, are being discussed or have already been implemented. In the EU, the inclusion of aviation in the emissions trading system has already led to a financial burden for airlines, but this is mostly passed on to consumers.

Corporate strategies

Some LCCs are starting to adapt their strategies to be perceived as more environmentally friendly. These include investments in more efficient aircraft, the use of biofuels and compensation programmes for air travel. However, these measures are often criticised as insufficient.

Social discourse

There is a growing social movement criticising air travel as a whole and LCCs in particular. Under hashtags such as #Flugscham ("Flight Shame"), consumers are called upon to rethink their travel habits and choose alternatives such as rail travel.

Future challenges

The pressure on LCCs to change their environmentally harmful practices is likely to increase. This poses a fundamental challenge to their business model, as more sustainable practices usually involve higher costs that are difficult to reconcile with the need to offer low ticket prices.

Social and cultural changes

LCCs have brought about profound cultural and social changes that affect the way people travel and live. The ability to fly at low cost has revolutionised the travel behaviour of the general population and created a culture of mobility and connectivity that would have been unthinkable a few decades ago.

Democratisation of travel

One of the main features of low-cost airlines is the democratisation of air travel. Flying is no longer the privilege of a wealthy elite; with low prices and a variety of routes, many more people have access to destinations across Europe and beyond.

Change in leisure time activities

The ability to fly cheaply has changed the way people spend their free time. Weekend trips to other countries have become the norm for many. This has also led to the popularisation of city breaks, where tourists fly to a city for a few days.

Effects on identity

Increased mobility also influences how people see themselves and their belonging to a particular culture or nation. The easy accessibility of other countries and cultures promotes a cosmopolitan worldview and broadens cultural horizons.

Social impact

Low-cost airlines have also helped families and friends who live in different countries through work or study to stay in touch more easily. At the same time, however, this has created an expectation that people will quickly fly to another country for birthdays, weddings or other important family events, which can create a certain social pressure.

Cultural homogenisation

Another aspect is the cultural homogenisation promoted by mass tourism. Local traditions and specificities can be diluted by the influx of tourists, which in turn reduces the cultural diversity of destinations.

Globalisation of the middle class

LCCs have in some ways contributed to the globalisation of the middle class. Cheap flights make the world a smaller place, and experiencing other cultures is no longer the preserve of the higher income classes. This also has implications for the global economy, as people are now more willing to spend money in other countries.

Political impact

Facilitated mobility can also have political consequences. For example, the possibility to travel across borders has contributed to more intense European integration and solidarity. On the other hand, the ease of travel can also complicate issues such as migration and border security.

Changed relationship with distances

LCCs have also changed our understanding of distances. What used to seem far away is now just a short flight away. This not only has an impact on our leisure time activities, but also on professional decisions. It is not uncommon today for people to commute regularly between different countries for their work.

Influencing self-esteem

In a world of social media, the ability to travel "anywhere" can also increase self-worth. Photos of exotic locations or popular cities are shared on platforms such as Instagram, which in turn increases the pressure to take such trips themselves.

Generational differences

Younger generations who have grown up with the availability of LCC often have a very different attitude towards travel than older generations. They take travel for granted and this also shapes their relationship to issues such as sustainability and climate change, which may be less of a focus for older generations.

Education and tolerance

Easier access to different cultures and places also promotes education and tolerance. People who have the opportunity to see different parts of the world often develop a more nuanced understanding of geopolitical and social issues.

In sum, the development of LCC has led to a complex set of cultural and social changes whose full impact is not yet fully understood. On the one hand, they have opened up numerous opportunities, but they also bring with them a number of challenges and responsibilities

Survival strategies

Sustainability

Research and development in low-emission technologies for aircraft are crucial elements in minimising the environmental impact of aviation. The pressure to develop such technologies comes from both regulatory authorities and an increasingly environmentally conscious public.

Hybrid and electric drives

One of the most promising developments are hybrid and electric engines for aircraft. Various companies and research institutes are working on developing powerful batteries and electric motors capable of powering an aircraft. These technologies are still at the experimental stage, but show great potential.

Fuel from renewable sources

Another way to reduce CO_2 emissions is to use sustainable aviation fuel derived from renewable sources such as vegetable oil or algae. Various airlines have already experimented with the use of these fuels and some flights are already partly operated with sustainable fuel.

Improvement of aerodynamics

Research in the field of aerodynamics aims to minimise the aerodynamic drag of aircraft in order to reduce fuel consumption. This can be achieved through design optimisations, such as the development of more efficient wing shapes.

Lightweight materials

The use of lightweight materials such as carbon fibre reinforced plastics (CFRP) can help to reduce the weight of aircraft and thus lower fuel consumption and CO_2 emissions.

Flight path optimisation

Modern technologies such as artificial intelligence and big data can be used to optimise flight routes. More efficient flight routes can save fuel and time, which in turn leads to a reduction in emissions.

Collaboration and partnerships

Close cooperation between aircraft manufacturers, aviation companies, research institutes and governments is needed to develop these technologies effectively. Various international organisations and agreements, such as the Paris Climate Agreement, also provide the framework for the development of low-emission technologies.

Public and private funding

The development of low-emission technologies requires considerable investment. Public funding as well as private investment play a crucial role in this. Only an efficient combination of public and private funding can provide the resources needed for research and development.

Overall, research and development in the field of low-emission technologies is a complex and interdisciplinary field involving a multitude of actors and factors. The challenge is to develop technologies that are not only more environmentally friendly, but also economically viable and safe to operate.

Future regulations and laws

Future regulations and legislation in the aviation industry, especially in the LCC segment, will play a crucial role in shaping the industry. They will bring both opportunities and challenges and will influence how LCCs adapt their business models to remain profitable while becoming more environmentally friendly.

Climate protection legislation

Given the global focus on climate protection, it is to be expected that strict emission reduction targets will be introduced. These could be realised in the form of CO_2

taxes, emissions trading schemes or mandatory use of sustainable fuels. For LCCs, this could mean an increased financial burden, which may be passed on to customers.

Consumer protection

In the area of consumer protection, there could be tightening to ensure transparency in ticket prices and easier enforcement of passenger rights. LCCs in particular, which often operate with additional charges, could be affected by this.

International air transport

Depending on geopolitical developments, there could be changes in the open skies agreements that regulate access to certain markets. For LCCs that are heavily dependent on cross-border traffic, this would be of great importance.

Data protection

In the digital age, data security and protection also play an increasingly important role. New regulations could affect the way airlines collect, store and use data, which in turn could impact customer loyalty and marketing.

Labour law

Stricter rules on working conditions and rights for airline employees could also be introduced. This would be particularly relevant for LCCs, where working conditions are often considered less favourable.

Regional policy and subsidies

Another interesting field is regional policy, especially the allocation of subsidies for airports or certain flight routes. Changes here could directly influence the route network of LCCs.

Sustainability goals and social responsibility

Last but not least, requirements for corporate social responsibility (CSR) could also increase, including the obligation to disclose sustainability reports.

In summary, future regulations and legislation will have a significant impact on the strategy, business model and profitability of LCCs. It will therefore be essential for these airlines to be able to react flexibly to changes and continuously adapt their business practices.

Post-COVID 19 trends

The COVID 19 pandemic has brought about profound changes in people's travel behaviour and thus also in the airline industry, including LCC. These changes range from the shift to digital technologies to a new focus on health and safety.

Health and safety

The pandemic has increased the focus on health and safety when travelling. Consumers now expect improved hygiene measures, contactless technologies and flexible booking options. LCCs have often had to follow suit to regain and maintain customer trust.

Demand for flexibility

The uncertainty created by travel restrictions and bans has led to consumers seeking more flexibility in bookings. This means that LCCs, which traditionally offered less flexible fares, now need to offer more diverse options such as free rebooking or refunds.

Emergence of domestic travel

While international travel has been restricted by border closures and quarantine requirements, interest in domestic travel has increased. Some LCCs have recognised this trend and adjusted their route networks accordingly.

Virtual meetings vs. business trips

With the rise of video conferencing and virtual meetings, the need for business travel has decreased. This may have a long-term impact on demand for air travel, including for LCCs, some of which also target business travellers.

Changes in booking behaviour

The pandemic has led to many people planning their trips at shorter notice, often due to uncertainties around travel restrictions. This presents a challenge for airlines' capacity planning and pricing.

Sustainability awareness

The pandemic has also raised awareness of sustainable travel. It is likely that travellers will increasingly choose airlines that are committed to protecting the environment. LCCs face the challenge of adapting their business model to meet this growing need.

Digitisation

The pandemic has highlighted the importance of digitalisation in the travel experience. From booking to check-in and boarding, airlines are increasingly turning to mobile and web-based solutions to minimise contact between staff and passengers.

What does the future hold?

Low-cost strategy of conventional airlines

In recent years, a remarkable transformation has taken place in the airline industry, driven primarily by the increasing presence of low-cost carriers. This has put considerable pressure on conventional airlines to rethink their business models and, in many cases, to adapt their offerings to those of low-cost competitors.

In the past, conventional airlines often enjoyed a monopoly or at least a dominant position in their respective markets. They could rely on a well-heeled clientele willing to pay for comfort and service. But the emergence of low-cost airlines has changed the rules of the game. These airlines score with low prices, which resonates especially with younger travellers and the budget-conscious.

In the course of this shift, traditional airlines are increasingly forced to become more flexible and adapt to changing customer behaviour. This is reflected above all in a more differentiated pricing policy. For example, many established airlines now offer fare options that are structured along the lines of low-cost offers. There are "basic economy" or "light" fares where ticket prices are lower but various restrictions apply, such as baggage check-in fees or limited seat selection. In this way, they try to appeal to a broader customer base without losing their premium customers, who continue to pay for amenities and comfort.

However, there are also pitfalls in this adaptation process. Traditional airlines must be careful not to dilute their brand identity. Striking a balance between cutting costs and maintaining a high-quality service is difficult. If they cut too many amenities, they risk losing their premium customers; if they fail to optimise their cost structure, they remain vulnerable to competition from low-cost carriers.

Most major European airlines are already going down this path, and it is likely to intensify and put further pressure on LCCs.

Newcomers from non-EU countries

There are many LCCs in the US and UK. Is there a risk that one day they will be allowed to fly within the EU as well?

The question of whether airlines from the UK or the US can fly within Europe is closely linked to international agreements, regulations and aviation legislation.

First, it is important to distinguish between domestic flights within a European country and flights between different European countries. Flights between European countries are usually permitted for airlines from third countries such as the US or the UK, provided there are bilateral agreements or multilateral treaties that allow this. For example, a US airline can offer a flight from New York to Frankfurt and then fly on to Rome, provided it has the necessary permits and slots.

Domestic flights within a European country (for example from Berlin to Munich) are a different matter. Such flights are usually referred to as "cabotage" and in many cases are restricted to foreign airlines. Within the European Union, it was long the case that any airline from an EU member state could operate cabotage flights in any other EU member state. This was part of the European Common Aviation Market.

The UK was part of this system until Brexit, but has been a third country since then. Currently, the conditions for flights between the UK and the EU, as well as any cabotage flights within the EU, are governed by the Trade and Cooperation Agreement between the EU and the UK. As a rule, cabotage flights are now no longer allowed for UK airlines within the EU, unless specific bilateral agreements are made.

US airlines are generally not permitted to operate cabotage flights within the EU, as the US is not part of the European Common Aviation Market. While there are extensive bilateral agreements between the EU and the US, these do not generally allow for the provision of domestic flights by each other.

Whether this will change one day - for example within the framework of trade agreements - is difficult to predict, but by no means impossible.

Long distance

The LCC business model is based on reducing operating costs and transferring these savings to customers in the form of cheaper ticket prices. However, most low-cost carriers focus mainly on short-haul flights, as this model is easier to apply to such distances. For short-haul flights, the flight duration is shorter, so fewer on-board amenities are required, which in turn reduces costs.

For long-haul flights, the situation is more complicated. First of all, operating costs are inherently higher for long-haul flights, from fuel costs to fees for using international airports and crew requirements, which often consist of more members and require more rest time. In addition, passengers on longer flights tend to expect more amenities such as better meals, in-flight entertainment and more comfortable seats, which also increase costs.

However, some low-cost carriers have tried to extend the low-cost model to long-haul flights. Norwegian Air Shuttle is an example of an airline that has tried to offer low-cost long-haul flights. However, Norwegian has experienced difficulties due to various challenges, including high operating costs and passenger expectations of higher service levels, and has discontinued this service. In Europe, FlyPlay is currently engaged there.

But there are also some success stories, albeit mostly in Asia. AirAsia X, a subsidiary of Malaysia's AirAsia, is an example of a successful low-cost long-haul airline, offering flights from Asia to Australia, the Middle East and even Hawaii. They have implemented a model where basic services are low cost, but extra services such as baggage, meals and seat selection cost extra.

It remains to be seen whether the low-cost model will be able to gain a lasting foothold on long-haul flights. So far, there have been both success stories and failures, and the dynamics of supply and demand, operating costs and passenger expectations continue to challenge the model.

Potential disruptors and their strategies

Potential disruptors in the LCC industry are companies or technologies that have the potential to significantly change or even displace established business models. Their strategies can be diverse and complex, but they often feature radical innovations or transformative business models.

Use of technology

For example, a potential disruptor could introduce a breakthrough technology in aviation or the passenger experience. This could range from using greener fuel alternatives to implementing virtual reality experiences for passengers.

Radical cost reduction

A new entrant could develop a business model that drastically reduces operating costs and thus ticket prices. This could be achieved through automation, outsourcing or other innovative approaches.

Networking and data use

A disruptive company could better personalise and optimise its services by using big data analytics and artificial intelligence. As a result, it could increase customer loyalty and outperform traditional airlines in terms of customer service.

Multimodal transport solutions

The integration of air services with other modes of transport such as trains, buses or car-sharing services could also be considered as a disruptive strategy. Such multimodal offers could improve travel efficiency and enable a seamless transition between different modes of transport.

Decentralisation and localisation

Instead of focusing on large transport hubs, a disruptor could pursue a strategy of decentralisation by serving smaller, less frequented airports. This could make travel more convenient and faster while reducing operating costs.

Change in distribution channels

The use of new or unconventional distribution channels, such as social media or blockchain-based ticketing platforms, could also be considered a disruptive strategy.

Partnerships outside the industry

Collaborations with companies in other sectors such as retail, entertainment or technology could open up new revenue streams and provide additional value to customers.

Social and environmental responsibility

A growing consumer focus on sustainability and social responsibility could also provide an opportunity for disruptors who invest in these aspects and integrate them into their business model.

Direct customer interaction

Disruptors could also use new forms of customer interaction and community building to build a loyal customer base, for example through gamification, loyalty programmes or other forms of customer engagement.

Adaptability and agility

Potential disruptors could react faster and more flexibly to market trends and customer needs due to their smaller company size and flatter hierarchies.

Overall, a potential disruptor in the LCC industry could challenge established companies through a combination of these strategies and approaches and significantly change the existing market structure. It is important to bear in mind that these companies must not only have innovative ideas, but also the resources and execution expertise to successfully implement their disruptive strategies.

Shift to rail

The shift of passenger traffic from air to rail is another potential disruptive change for the LCC industry. This is particularly relevant in Europe, where the rail network is well developed and distances between major cities are relatively short. Consumers' increasing environmental awareness may make rail travel more attractive as a greener alternative to air travel. Trains emit significantly less CO_2 per passenger-kilometre compared to planes.

The EU and individual European countries could take policy measures to encourage the shift from air to rail. This could be done, for example, by introducing CO_2 taxes, increasing airport taxes or direct subsidies for rail transport. The same applies to an immediate legal ban on short-haul flights if rail connections are available.

For short to medium distance journeys, rail transport can be competitive or even superior in terms of time in many cases, especially when taking into account the time for check-in, security checks and boarding for air travel. Trains often take passengers directly to city centres, while airports are usually located outside and add additional time and cost for transfers to the final destination.

New developments such as high-speed trains and Maglev (maglev) technology could make rail travel even faster and more comfortable, making it more attractive than air travel.

In addition to environmental awareness, social trends such as "slow travel" could also contribute to people choosing rail as a more pleasant and relaxed travel option.

The combination of these factors could lead to rail transport in Europe becoming a serious competitor to LCCs for certain routes and target groups. For carriers, this could mean rethinking their business models and possibly focusing more on longer routes or specialised market segments that are less susceptible to a shift to rail

Conclusion and outlook

The future outlook for low-cost carriers (LCCs) is promising overall, but they also face a number of challenges that they must overcome in order to be successful in the long term. The travel industry is inherently volatile and can be affected by a variety of factors, such as economic fluctuations, geopolitical events or pandemics. In addition, competition is increasing, both among low-cost carriers themselves and with traditional airlines, which are also trying to become more cost-efficient.

Here are some aspects that low-cost carriers should consider to improve their future prospects:

Adaptability: The ability to adapt quickly to changing market conditions is crucial. Whether it's adjusting prices or introducing new routes, flexibility can be a big advantage.

Diversification: Expanding the offering beyond just air service can be an important source of revenue. Some low-cost carriers already offer hotel bookings, car rentals or even train tickets to increase revenue.

Customer experience: Although price is often the deciding factor in choosing a low-cost carrier, a good customer experience can help increase customer loyalty. Simple booking systems, friendly service and reliability are key components here.

Sustainability: Given the growing awareness of the environmental impact of air travel, sustainability is becoming an increasingly important factor. Airlines that invest in environmentally friendly technologies or offset their CO_2 emissions could have a competitive advantage.

Technology: The integration of modern technologies can increase efficiency and reduce costs. Whether it's improved booking systems, advanced algorithms for revenue management or IoT applications to monitor aircraft health, technology will play a crucial role.

Long-haul models: The expansion of the low-cost model to long-haul flights remains a challenge, but also offers opportunities for growth. However, airlines need to find a balance between cost efficiency and passengers' higher expectations for comfort and service on long-haul flights.

Regulations and partnerships: Finally, LCCs should also keep an eye on the regulatory framework. Regulatory compliance, especially in terms of safety and environmental requirements, as well as the ability to partner with other airlines or service providers, can be crucial.

Low-cost carriers have already proven that they can be disruptive and shake up the air transport market. However, to continue to be successful, they need to remain innovative, continuously adapt their business models and respond to the changing needs and expectations of customers.

There is little doubt that most will succeed.

Made in United States
North Haven, CT
02 December 2023

Made in United States
North Haven, CT
02 December 2023